DO IT T[...]

15 Ways to Step up to Life by Stepping Outside Your Comfort Zone

By

Marc Mulligan

ISBN: 9781520186467 (Paperback)

www.outsidethecomfortzone.ie

I dedicate this book to my parents Margo & Fintan and my partner Csilla. You guys are my motivation. Thank you.

WARNING: This book is here to motivate readers to step outside of their comfort zones and challenge themselves. Some ways of stepping outside the comfort zone involve physical challenges or risks. If you decide to undertake any challenges or risks which could endanger you, you must ensure to take all possible safety measures. This includes getting advice from experts and using the correct equipment. The author cannot be held responsible for any accidents or injuries that occur. Be smart, be safe.

The author also cannot be held responsible for how awesome you become as you put into action the words on the following pages. You will be completely responsible for that because you're the one stepping outside your comfort zone. Well done you!

CONTENTS

Introduction:

Why You Need to Step Outside Your Comfort Zone

"F.E.A.R. – False Evidence Appearing Real"

I stepped outside of my comfort zone. It changed my life. I now have better focus, more confidence, I'm more productive, I'm more creative, I have a greater sense of control and I adapt to change more easily.

Many authors will thank you for buying their book - I will receive my reward if you apply the advice it contains. And so I thank you, in advance, for completing the challenges prepared for you in the following chapters. I am grateful for your focus. Focus is something that has become more difficult to find in recent years. Many people I know, educated and intelligent people, are unable to read books. They just cannot commit to a longer focus of their attention. If your focus does wane, please, stick with it. It will be worth it, I promise.

Stepping outside your comfort zone is known to be one of the best things you can do for yourself. But why? With this book I will clarify exactly WHY it is so good for us and HOW we can go about using this strategy to better ourselves. I can tell you because I have lived *inside* and *outside* the comfort zone. I know the difference and what is involved.

I am not a psychologist nor do I have any official qualifications in study of the mind or human nature of any kind. I studied film and television production at college. I then went on to work in banking. You know, a typical career progression.

1

Nor do I think I have all the answers. I still have so much learning to do. But I *know* that this works. I have a set out a system for it in this book.

I am fascinated by the subject of fear and of challenging ourselves. My interest in, and my knowledge of, this subject are spawned from my own experiences, my own research, listening to others speak about their experiences and my own observations. A key message that I wish to instil in you is the fact that all fears and challenges stem from one thing: *Fear of the Unknown*.

My mission is to encourage more and more people to increase their self-awareness about how fear affects them and what to do about it. Most of us are completely unaware of the effect fear has on us.

The reason is simple. I have lived most of my life until recent years comfortably safe within my comfort zone. For the first 28 years of my life I only ever played it safe. I unconsciously assessed every situation and always took the safest option. I wasn't even aware that I was doing this until a good friend pointed it out to me. At the time I reacted defensively (which is another way of remaining inside the comfort zone) but in the weeks following what he said, I gave it more thought. He was right. I was on permanent play-it-safe mode. Look where it had gotten me: a boring, unsatisfying job and not enough time or energy in my free time to do anything interesting or anything of any worth with my life. I was unsatisfied, unfulfilled and physically, mentally and spiritually decaying. I was only a young man in my twenties yet my friend, mentioned above, said I behaved like an old man. That was a difficult thing to hear from a close friend, especially because it was true.

What was the end result from always playing it safe?: Crippling stress and anxiety which compromised every decision I made in my life and ultimately lead to a traumatic brain injury. I was out sick from work for 2 years as a result of this brain injury. During that time I did not know how to recover, how long it would take to fully recover or even if I would ever recover and be able to have a normal life at all.

I don't think I'm the only one either. In many parts of the world we are becoming more complacent about our lives. Too many things are handed to us on a plate. What happens when that plate is suddenly taken away? When the worldwide financial crash

2

happened in 2008, we experienced a taste of it. Too many people are living their entire lives within their comfort zones and not being fully aware of other aspects of their lives, including their physical and mental health, as a result.

And it's not only in first world countries. It's obvious in the first world but it happens everywhere. Think of a twenty year old who lives in an economically weak country. They may be hardworking and clever but opportunity will typically be harder to find in their country. So what do many of them do? They step outside their comfort zones by leaving their home country and setting up in another country, usually a better developed country with better economic prospects for them. Is it an easy transition for them? Very unlikely. It means leaving the culture, the way of life, the friends and family who they grew up with. But is it worthwhile to do? Maybe not in literally every case but in many, many cases for these individuals their quality of life is much, much better if they are able to adapt to the new culture, the new people, the new way of life.

It's so easy for us to be sucked back into our comfort zones without even realising it. We slip into our routines. For example: Wake up > work > dinner > television > bed.
When we live inside a relentless routine we lose our chance at ever making an impact with our life.

Stepping outside of your comfort zone is the *only* way you will ever know what it is that you are capable of doing. You can go through your life safely ticking all the necessary boxes, doing the minimum that you are required to do or… you can *really live* by consciously deciding to do what you thought you could not do.

It is the very thing that you are weakest at that you benefit the most from doing. You'll be destroying your self-limiting beliefs (we'll come back to self-limiting beliefs later) and at the same time improving your range of skills, or your fitness level or your mental agility. You'll also see faster returns on your effort than someone who has been doing that thing for months or years already. For example, if you've never done consistent physical training: do it today. You may not look like a rock star immediately but you will *feel* like a rock star in just a few weeks. The people who I have worked with on the Outside the Comfort Zone System have told me that they felt like "heroes" and "rock stars" even halfway through it.

3

You can spend your life doing things which never truly challenge you, never truly make you feel alive. It's your life. Your choice. But if you are being honest with yourself you know the things which don't make you a stronger, more effective, more fulfilled person. Just think of the things that you allow to fill up time in your life which don't improve your situation. We all have them: channel surfing the television, drinking alcohol too much and too often, wasting time on random online searches, playing video games for long stretches of time. There are a myriad of other activities like these. None of these things need to be a problem for you but when we spend a significant amount of time at them, of course they are a problem for you.

When I speak about stepping outside the comfort zone I'm not only talking about physical challenges such as running a race or climbing a mountain. I'm talking about everything that you feel you are not able to do or that you are afraid of trying. The only exceptions being the things that are harmful to you or to others, things which we all know would be destructive or unhelpful. Think: quitting smoking, learning how to type properly, conquering your weakest subject at school, public speaking, handling a snake or a spider, learning a language, starting your own business or even just switching that phone off for 24 hours.

What I have achieved in the few years since my recovery from brain trauma is something which I never would have thought myself capable of. I had always been terrified of public speaking. Now I frequently speak to a variety of audiences. I have been privileged to work with tens of thousands of people since I began delivering my message. The people in my audiences and in my workshops are welcoming, hardworking, clever and creative. I have noticed a powerful curiosity, a willingness to learn. In fact, I also learn at these events. Often I learn just as much from them as they do from me.

Sharing my story, and the lessons I have learned, is my purpose. I try my best to emphasise the importance of stepping outside the comfort zone every time I get in front of the microphone or work closely with smaller groups. I try my best to give them the best because time is precious. Focus is precious. And our dreams are precious.

Look, I know stepping outside of your comfort zone can be scary. But the more you do it, the more your brain rewires itself and the more easily it comes to you the next time.

In my live presentations to audiences I reveal some of my most personal moments, my most vulnerable weaknesses in the hope that my audiences will learn from the mistakes that I made. I hope that you too will learn from my story so that you don't have to go through what I had to go through to learn it.

Of all the ways there are to step outside of your comfort zone, the most important are the ones you already know. The tasks and projects and actions that you have been putting off until now. Do it today.

If you are ready to step up to this challenge, the challenge of stepping outside your comfort zone, turn to the next page.

Do it <u>today</u>.

1. Stepping Outside the Comfort Zone

"True bravery is not absence of fear
but action in the face of fear."

The title of this book "Do It Today" I believe has great importance for everyone. From Buddhist monks to wise modern educators, the mantra "Do it today" is just as important now, if not more than in the past. Every day we are assaulted with so many different things looking for our attention. Tasks to complete at home or at work, advertisements screaming at us, technology and other people who want to engage with us. The only way to know for sure that you are doing anything constructive or making any progress in your life is to do it today. "Tomorrow" really means "Never".

The subtitle: "15 Ways to Step Up to Life By Stepping Outside Your Comfort Zone" refers to the Outside the Comfort Zone System which is positioned in the final chapter of this book. Every page between here and there is designed to prepare you to make the most of the Outside the Comfort Zone System. All the various parts of the system have been tested, developed and refined by me with small and large groups of participants. I am so excited for you to try it for yourself.

There are a lot of authors and speakers out there who promise that they have the answer for you. The answer to how to achieve more in your life. The answer to how to be happier. The answer to what is your life's meaning. These are big promises. In many cases, they are not followed through.

There are three steps in providing these difficult answers. 1) Teaching what you, the reader or listener, need to understand. 2) Describing how you can take action by providing a plan or a system. 3) Keeping you motivated to take that action.

Many authors and speakers cover parts 1 & 2 perfectly but fall down on part 3. There are some who are the other way around, they are good at providing an action plan and some motivation to take action but do not communicate what exactly the purpose of it is.

This book has been written and rewritten with the reader in mind. The words are for people of all ages, in any culture, country and with, or without, any religion. If you have ever hesitated to speak your mind, to offer your ideas at a business meeting or to your boss. If you have ever told yourself that you cannot resolve that mathematical problem at school. If you have ever regretted not approaching that special someone you liked and now it is too late. If you are retired from your career and you wish you had made more if your life. This book is for you.

I want you to understand, inside out, exactly what I am saying, exactly what you need to do next and I want you to be motivated to put it into action. Without all 3 elements, there is no point in me writing or you reading this book.

The majority of self help books are read with interest… and then placed back on a bookshelf (or just forgotten on an electronic device) and never read again and never actioned. So, for a moment, the reader is inspired to take control of their life but that only lasts a moment. So what is the point?

If there is something in this book which does not make sense to you I urge you to get in touch, I am happy to clarify anything for you. I want you to make the most of this book. I want you to have the very best that you can have and be the very best that you can be.

You can reach me at marc@outsidethecomfortzone.ie

I firmly believe that the reason why so many of us do not have the possessions, the experiences and the life that we desire is that we are not willing to step outside of our comfort zones in order to obtain them. Everything you ever really want to bring into your life is just outside your comfort zone. This book provides a plan for managing your ventures outside of your comfort zone, allowing you obtain what you want in a structured and proven way.

The earliest mention I could find of the expression "Outside the Comfort Zone" was in a study conducted in 1908 by Robert M. Yerkes and John D. Dodson. In the study they discovered that stimulation improved performance of the mice test subjects... up to a certain point. When that point was passed, when the poor mice were under too much stress, their performance deteriorated. *(http://psychclassics.yorku.ca/Yerkes/Law/)*

That 1908 study clarified something which most of us are aware of already: that pressure or stress, up to a certain point, is helpful in improving our performance but when we are pushed too hard, our performance is weaker. It's something that teachers, parents and students can testify to all too easily. Parents and teachers are often aware that too much pressure can harm their children or students' results. Finding the correct balance is the challenge.

Behavioral scientist and business thinker Daniel H. Pink says "We need a place of productive discomfort. If you're too comfortable, you're not productive. And if you're too uncomfortable, you're not productive. Like Goldilocks, we can't be too hot or too cold." *(Drive: The Surprising Truth About What Motivates Us, Daniel H. Pink, 2009)*

In my own understanding, stepping outside the comfort zone means being challenged. You may find yourself being pushed outside your comfort zone by others or by circumstances beyond your control or you may be challenging yourself. You might do it because you want to grow as a person. Or because you can see something or someone that you want which you know cannot be reached as long as you remain inside your comfort zone. Or maybe you are simply looking for a challenge. Regardless of why you are stepping outside your comfort zone, every time you do it, you grow, you become stronger, more confident. Your ability to handle challenging situations and problems in the future increases.

It is perfectly normal and logical that we strive to avoid problems and conflict in our everyday lives. If we didn't, we would be beset with disaster after disaster. As a result It may be counterintuitive for many of us to go looking for challenges to overcome because a challenge is just another word for a problem, right? But we must face existing challenges and problems otherwise we ignore them and they become worse or the problem spreads to others like a disease. One way to face existing problems or challenges is to look more closely at ourselves. Many of us shy away from looking into our own true motives, desires and dreams. I will guide you with this in detail in the final chapter of this book.

We can take it even further by actively looking for challenges. Many thrill seekers actively look for challenges by finding new waves to surf and new mountains to climb. These people are a great example to the rest of us. But these great physical challenges are not for everyone. Your challenges and achievements may lie elsewhere. We can seek and find challenges to overcome in *every* aspect of our lives: Health, Fitness, Career, Money, Living Environment, Family, Friends, Romance, Mind, Spirit, Creativity & Personal Development.

As an inventor, Thomas Edison made 1,000 (some say 10,000) unsuccessful attempts at inventing the light bulb (the exact figure has been lost in the mists of time). When a reporter asked, *"How did it feel to fail 1,000 times?"* Edison replied, *"I didn't fail 1,000 times. I learned 1,000 ways how NOT to make a light bulb."*

When I first heard this story about Thomas Edison, I thought that it was silly. Edison had simply changed the wording around for his response. I wasn't impressed. However, when I thought about it a little more, I realised that not only was the wording different, the perspective was different and that was much more significant. Edison did not allow himself to feel like a failure. If he had felt like a failure, he would have quit after the first, or second or at most, the tenth attempt. He kept picking himself back up and trying again and again. He would not accept failure.

Adversity shapes us for better and for worse..

The past can weigh down on us. The big events in our lives, the terrible events in our lives, the ones which more impact they had at the time, they can weigh us down like anchors. But even those of us with the heaviest anchors are not cursed to be weighed down by them forever. We have a choice. The first thing to accept is that we DO have a choice. Once we accept that, we can then make the choice. Hopefully we make the choice to free ourselves from the anchors. Once we have done that, we are free to be present in the now where we are at our happiest and at our most effective.

When we fail to take action because of fear, we eventually become paralyzed in that area of our life. It can also spread to other areas of our life. This paralysis leads to anxiety. The thing that we have been avoiding due to fear, even if we didn't really know it was fear, has taken control of a small or big part of our life.

Exercise:

Here's something to try right now: *Do something that challenges you now.*

It could be something tiny or something big (although usually more preparation is required for a big challenge). Find something you can do right now that you have been avoiding. You may need to think creatively to come up with something. Call that person you like and ask them out or book that dental appointment or get out for a run (even it's raining and the middle of the night!) or tidy that mess in the bedroom that you never seem to get around to doing. If you can't think of anything right now just do something silly. For example, see how long you can stand on one foot. It requires focus. Time yourself.

A few years ago I lived near a hill. I wasn't in great physical shape at the time. I used to get up out of bed in the morning and before my brain could begin to question "Should I do this?" "But what if I can't run the whole way?" "What if I'm too tired to function at the office later?", I bolted out the door and ran up that hill.. It was so much easier to do because my mind was not resisting it. If I had tried it in the afternoon or evening, a part of my mind would have stopped me. It would have asked "Can I really do this?" And the answer would have come before I even had a chance to think about it. The answer would have been "No, of course not, are you crazy?"
By doing it first thing in the morning, I managed to side step the self-doubting, over-thinking that I and so many other people suffer with. After accomplishing something first thing in the morning, I felt in control for the rest of the day, I was better prepared for any challenges that came my way.

Find your own hill and climb it, first thing in the morning. If you're not a morning person, it might just mean getting up and out of bed 5 minutes early instead of hitting the snooze button!

2. What is Fear?

*"Many people die at 25
but are not buried until they're 75."*

Dictionary Definition of Fear: *"a distressing emotion aroused by impending danger, evil, pain, etc. whether the threat is real or imagined; the feeling or condition of being afraid."* (Dictionary.com)

Dictionary Definition of Phobia: *"a persistent, irrational fear of a specific object, activity, or situation that leads to a compelling desire to avoid it."* (Dictionary.com)

Mythological: Phobos represents <u>fear</u> in <u>Greek mythology</u>. He was the son of <u>Aphrodite</u> and <u>Ares</u>. He was known for going into battle with Ares. Greek poet Hesiod depicted Phobos on the shield of Heracles as "…staring backwards with eyes that glowed with fire. His mouth was full of teeth in a white row, fearful and daunting…"

A phobia is a more intense version of a fear. Nothing more. We do not all suffer from phobias, but we all experience fear (an exception to this fact is described later in this chapter) and we are all controlled to different extents by our fears whether we are conscious of them or not.

Fear is most often caused by your mind asking the question *"Can I handle this situation?"* and believing that you cannot handle it. The simple truth is that the more we put ourselves into these situations which we thought we could not handle, the less unnecessary fear we feel. In turn, the more situations that we *know* we can handle. This book you hold in your hands (or on your device) right now will guide you through this process.

The Science of Fear

Let's take a brief overview of how fear works biologically.

Fear is caused by experiencing a sudden fright or feeling like you are in a situation that you cannot handle. We'll call this the trigger. Fear is an unconscious process, in other words we do not need to think about the process in order for it to happen, it's automatic.

Once fear is triggered, two processes are activated in the brain:

The Low Road

The low road which is a quick, emergency response and the high road which is slower but interprets events in more detail. Both of these processes happen at the same time. The low road is your immediate reaction, before all the information is in. If you see someone over-reacting to a threat, that's the low road in action.

While the low road is working away, the high road is already looking deeper into the details. Is it really a threat or not?

The High Road

The high road takes longer but is a more reliable process.
If a friend jumps out in front of you disguised as a ghost, the second or two where you panic, that's the low road. Adrenaline surges, you're ready to act fast. The panic ends a moment later because the high road has assessed the situation in the meantime and decided that there is no threat.

The hypothalamus is the part of the brain that controls the fight or flight response. When the fear message reaches it, it reacts by activating the sympathetic nervous system and the adrenal-cortical system.

The sympathetic nervous system causes the body and brain to act faster and become alert. It causes the stress hormones adrenaline and noradrenaline to be released into the bloodstream.

When the adrenal-cortical system is activated, it causes the release of another 30 hormones which all make the body and mind more alert and focused.

The release of all of these hormones forces many reactions in your body and brain:

- Non-essential organs stop functioning to leave more energy for this emergency.
- Small details become ignored while the brain focuses heavily on the main threat.
- Your blood-glucose level is increased.
- Your pupils dilate so that you can see as well as possible.
- Blood pressure and heart rate increases.
- Your veins constrict in order to redirect additional blood to your main muscle groups. This is the cause for that feeling of the hairs on the back of your neck standing up.
- Your muscles tense up.

Urbach-Wiethe Disease

There are people who have incurred damage to the amygdala part of the brain and as a result they cannot experience fear. The genetic condition Urbach-Wiethe disease affects only 400 people on the planet. A woman living in the U.S. code named SM kindly submitted herself for tests so that scientists and doctors could better understand the condition. What is known is that Urbach-Wiethe disease deteriorates the amygdala part of the brain leaving the sufferer with no ability to experience fear according to a study published in Current Biology in December 2010. In some ways that's a wonderful thing. Imagine all of the time and effort that she has NOT wasted worrying about things that will never happen in the future like most of the rest of us.

Study coauthor Justin Feinstein of the University of Iowa stated that "What that suggests to us is that perhaps the amygdala is acting at a very instinctual, unconscious level. Without the amygdala, instead of just losing your interest in things, you do the very thing that's opposite. She tends to approach the very things she should be avoiding."
The study's authors can't dismiss other brain regions' roles in experiencing fear. Yet SM's complete inability to experience the emotion — in a wide variety of forms — highlights the amygdala's pivotal role in feeling afraid.

The downside of not being able to experience fear is illustrated in what SM told a researcher a few years ago: "I was walking to the store, and I saw this man on a park bench. He said, 'Come here please.' So I went over to him. I said, 'What do you need?' He grabbed me by the shirt, and he held a knife to my throat and told me he was going to cut me. I told him -- I said, 'Go ahead and cut me.' And I said, 'I'll be coming back, and I'll hunt you down.' Oops. Was I supposed to say that? I'm sorry... I wasn't afraid. And for some reason, he let me go. And I walked home, instead of running."

A dangerous situation made even more dangerous by the fact that SM did not act with any caution. She could have died because of her lack of fear. The only positive here is that when the threat had passed she didn't have any lasting trauma, because the event had failed to faze her.

(https://www.washingtonpost.com/news/speaking-of-science/wp/2015/01/20/meet-the-woman-who-cant-feel-fear)

Fear Conditioning

The fear reaction has evolved over a very long period of time. But fear can also be conditioned, instilled into a person by their experiences. This fact is sometimes used by people in positions of power in order to increase their control of others.

"Little Albert was a 9-month-old infant who was tested on his reactions to various stimuli by Watson and Raynor (1920). He was shown a white rat, a rabbit, a monkey and various masks. Albert described as "on the whole stolid and unemotional" showed no fear of any of these stimuli. However, what did startle him and cause him to be afraid was if a hammer was struck against a steel bar behind his head. The sudden loud noise would cause "little Albert to burst into tears".

When Little Albert was 11 months old the white rat was presented and seconds later the hammer was struck against the steel bar. This was done 7 times over the next 7 weeks and each time Little Albert burst into tears. By now little Albert only had to see the rat and he immediately showed every sign of fear. He would cry (whether or not the hammer was hit against the steel bar) and he would attempt to crawl away.

In addition, the Watson and Rayner study found that Albert developed phobias of objects which shared characteristics with the rat; including the family dog, a fur coat, some cotton wool and a Santa Claus mask! This process is known as generalization.

Watson and Rayner had shown that classical conditioning could be used to create a phobia. Over the next few weeks and months Little Albert was observed and 10 days after conditioning his fear of the rat was much less marked." *(http://www.simplypsychology.org)*

"Psychologist Martin Seligman performed a classical conditioning experiment in which he showed subjects pictures of certain objects and then administered an electric shock. The idea was to create a phobia (an intense, irrational fear) of the object in the picture. When the picture was of something like a spider or a snake, it took only two to four shocks to establish a phobia. When the picture was of something like a flower or a tree, it took a lot more shocks to get a real fear going." *(How Stuff Works, 2005)*

Some fears are specific to only some, or one, cultures, communities or individuals. If you live in a high crime neighbourhood, you may have heard more stories about people being mugged, and therefore you, and others in your neighbourhood, will have a higher fear of being mugged.

"There is a phobia called *taijin kyofusho* that is considered in the psychiatric community to be a "culturally distinctive phobia in Japan." *Taijin kyofusho* is "the fear of offending other persons by an excess of modesty or showing respect." The intricate social rituals that are part of life in Japan have led to a Japanese-specific fear."

(http://science.howstuffworks.com/life/inside-the-mind/emotions/fear.htm)

Why Fear Can be Helpful

Before we continue I want to state that there are some situations where fear is helpful. In fact there are three clear ways in which it works for us.

1. Sometimes it's our unconscious mind telling us that danger is present when our conscious mind is not paying enough attention (otherwise known as gut instinct). Sometimes the temporary adrenaline rush provided by fear will help us to escape a real threat or help us to help others to escape a real threat.

Thousands of years ago, even just hundreds of years ago, fear was a much more useful thing. Imagine yourself as a prehistoric human creeping through a strange forest looking for sustenance. You come across a cave. There may be animals to kill and eat in that cave. As you approach the cave your instinctual fear kicks in. You have a feeling that it would be a bad idea to enter that cave. Maybe you subconsciously smelled something that you associate with dangerous animals or you heard something subtle without consciously realising it. Whatever it is, you feel fear. You back away and find another spot to hunt small animals. Later, you pass by that same cave again. As you near it, you see a large bear and its family of equally large bears exit the cave. You didn't have concrete information but your gut instinct saved you. Subtle details, which your conscious mind was not aware of, guided your decision to not enter the cave. Fear saved you.

In our world today, a modern equivalent to the example above can happen. A dark alleyway in the city. A person with a knife hiding from view in the shadows. We don't consciously detect him but something seems not right, so we don't enter the alleyway.

Unfortunately for SM, the lady with Urbach-Wiethe disease, she does not experience this gut feeling.

2. Fear can give us a better understanding of ourselves. When we experience fear it is often an instant unconscious reaction to a situation. For example: When someone sees a spider. If you have a fear of spiders, or arachnophobia, you are almost certainly aware

that you have it. If you feel fear or discomfort near spiders, then you have it. Like most things in life it works on a scale. You may have only a slight fear of spiders or your fear might be overwhelming. Either way, as with many fears, it's clear that you suffer from it. Great! You've learned something about yourself, some way in which you can become stronger. It may not seem like much of a consolation but if you want to be a more effective human being, it really is a benefit to know these things about ourselves.

3. It can help to focus us in times when focus is required.

In this book I will be encouraging you to step outside your comfort zone more and more in EVERY aspect of your life. Sometimes in ways you may not have even considered before. But in every case, I must be clear: Always be aware of the risks. Always take the correct precautions. Always take care in everything that you do. Climbing a tree to overcome your fear of heights is a wonderful thing which will make you a stronger person. However, climbing a tree after too many beers and using that drunken "dutch courage" to do it is not clever nor is it brave. It's just stupid and needlessly dangerous. You *must* continue to use your common sense.

Fear can occur whether or not there is a tangible physical threat present or not. Most of the time when we feel fear it is not caused by a physical threat. It is, most of the time, in our minds.

There are rational and irrational fears. A rational fear is where there is a real threat involved. For example, if you encountered a snake while out for a hike in the Amazon rainforest. If you feel fear in this case, it is warranted because, assuming you are not a snake expert, any snake you encounter could pose a threat to your health or even your life. An irrational fear is where there is no threat involved… at least not in the conventional sense. If you experience an irrational fear you are experiencing the same rush of adrenaline and the same fight or flight state of mind that some experiencing a rational fear does. For example, if you have a fear of the colour green most other people will not be able to relate to your fear. They may think you are crazy or joking. But irrational fears are just as real. And they can be just as difficult to overcome. The most recent irrational fears to appear on the Outside the Comfort Zone Fear Survey include helianthophobia - fear of sunflowers, pittakionophobia - fear of stickers and altocelarophobia - fear of high ceilings.

Many people live in a constant state of fear. We can become so used to the feeling of fear that we actually forget that we are experiencing it. Wouldn't it be like having an enormous weight be lifted from your shoulders to first discover that you have been afraid and then to remove that fear? The first step is to try to be more aware of when you experience fear. It may only be a low level of fear or an extreme phobia.

There are more obvious fears such as fear of heights (acrophobia) and less obvious fears such as fear of failure (atychiphobia), fear of change (metathesiophobia) and fear of the unknown (xenophobia). When we have a fear of heights we tend to know it. But when we have a fear like fear of failure we don't always acknowledge it. From my experience in working with audiences and individuals, my opinion is that *when we do not acknowledge a fear, it has an even greater effect on us.* Many people go through their entire lives without admitting fears or challenges to themselves. And that means that those fears and challenges nag at them, chase them relentlessly. The ones to watch out for are fear of failure, fear of chance and mostly: fear of the unknown.

By avoiding acknowledging our fears we only make them stronger.

We all need to step outside our comfort zones by looking more closely at ourselves… If there is a secret to all of this, it's that it is worth stepping outside of your comfort zone.

3. The Benefits of Stepping Outside your Comfort Zone

"Do the thing we fear, and death of fear is certain."
– Ralph Waldo Emerson

The benefits of stepping outside your comfort zone are many. You'll only fully experience them once you begin to challenge yourself. Here are some of the more important ones:

1. Increased productivity

Those who take more risks are far more productive in their work and personal lives. They have a momentum which can only be found by living on the edge or even just in the relative vicinity of the edge. However, being constantly on the edge is really not necessary.

2. Better focus - easier to remember and easier to understand concepts

"Concentrate all your thoughts upon the work at hand. The sun's rays do not burn until brought to a focus." - Alexander Graham Bell

"It's not that I'm so smart, it's just that I stay with problems longer." – Albert Einstein

Challenging situations require sharper focus. The more we put ourselves into challenging situations the more we train our focus. Focus is a much more difficult thing to find these days. Lots of people cannot focus long enough to read a book. I guess it's just a teething stage for our civilisation where we are the first few generations to be using advanced computer, phone and entertainment technology, all of which are exceptional at grabbing our attention and exceptional at reducing our ability to focus on other things.

3. Calmer - relaxed, not lazy

Have you ever been in a tough situation and then afterwards you felt relief and exhilaration? You may have felt calmer after you handled that tough situation than you did before it. The more you step outside your comfort zone the more you will experience this increased calmness at times of rest or in between your challenges.

4. A sense of control - of yourself & of any situation

If you know you can handle a difficult situation then you know you are well in control in more day to day ordinary situations.

5. Reduced resistance to change - change is *inevitable*

"It is not the strongest of the species, nor the most intelligent that survive. It is the one that is most adaptable to change". - Charles Darwin

Change is the most inevitable thing in life. Sometimes it seems like nothing is changing but that's only because the change is happening beneath the surface. Whether you are in a good situation right now or a bad one, it's going to change. The more you put yourself out there, into challenging situations, the more you train yourself to roll with change and make the changes work to your advantage.

6. Improved creativity - with self-expression, problem solving and sense of humour

Creativity is all about taking risks. What will they think of me once they hear this song I wrote? What will people say about this picture I drew? Am I funny or just embarrassing? Creativity increases the more you challenge yourself because you learn that risks are alright to take. In challenging situations we need to be creative to solve a problem.

7. Confidence to handle any situation - socialising, with colleagues, with clients, giving a presentation, at an exam, in an interview.

This is one of the more obvious benefits of stepping outside the comfort zone. Of course the more you prove to yourself that you can handle different situations, the more confidence you will have in any given situation.

8. Self-Reliance

There are many of us who are overly reliant on others. We don't push ourselves enough because we know we can just fall back on family or partners or friends. But we owe it to ourselves to be self-reliant... everyone who physically and mentally can be self-reliant needs to be. Every time you prove to yourself that you can overcome a challenge by yourself you become less reliant on others.

9. Increased presence

Eckhart Tolle extols the virtues of living in the present moment in his lectures and books. *The past is history, the future a mystery*. The present is the only thing that's real. It's the only time in which you can do or achieve anything in this life. But many of us spend our lives reliving the past and worrying about the future. Such a massive waste of time and effort. Every time you are outside your comfort zone you are forced into the present moment because you need to pay attention to what is happening right now in order to overcome the challenge. Live in the now.

10. Feeling more alive - more energy and clearer thinking

The more I challenged myself since my brain trauma, the more alive I have felt. In fact I have never felt this alive before. You may know what I mean by this. If you don't, you will know as soon as you start challenging yourself.

11. Overcoming fears - Even the ones you didn't know you had!

Your self-awareness will increase. Your awareness of what things are challenging for you and what fears you suffer from will become clearer. We need to know these things before we can overcome them. Most arachnophobia sufferers know that they have a fear of spiders but most atychiphobia (fear of failure) sufferers have no idea that they have a fear of failure. The more subtle fears such as fear of failure, fear of change, fear of success and most importantly: fear of the unknown are as sneaky as they are manipulative. They determine a huge amount of what we do and what we avoid doing. They are especially effective in controlling us when we are NOT aware of them... which for most of us is most of the time.

12. Learning more about yourself, how your mind works and what you really want in life

The more you work through a list of challenges for yourself, the more you'll discover what makes you tick. What drives you? What matters to you the most? And when you know these things, then you have even more reason to better yourself every day because you know what it is you are striving to achieve, to retain or to gain.

The list above covers a number of positives for you, however, the only way for you to really, truly see the benefits are for you to step outside of your own comfort zone.

It is easy for us to hear or read good advice, nod our heads and think *"Yeh, that makes sense, definitely the right thing to do"* and then proceed to NOT do it. There is a huge difference between intellectually knowing something and actually knowing it from

DOING it. I heard a good example of this using honey. If you had never tried honey and you asked a friend what it tastes like they might say that it is sweet, syrupy, sticky. Ok, that's helpful. But it's not the full picture. We only get the full picture when we actually taste the honey ourselves. It's the exact same thing with stepping outside your comfort zone. But stepping outside the comfort zone is far more beneficial to your life than tasting honey (sorry honey fans).

There are 15 excellent opportunities for you to step outside of your comfort zone at the end of this book. And these 15 opportunities all lead on to greater and more demanding challenges and opportunities which will push you as far as you are prepared to go. You alone will determine which direction these challenges and opportunities take.

4. The Benefits of Remaining Inside the Comfort Zone

5. Is Fear Really So Bad?

"Fear comes from uncertainty. When we are absolutely certain of our worth or our worthlessness, we are impervious to fear."
- **William Congreve**

The short answer is yes. I have described the few ways in which fear can be helpful in Chapter 2. Mostly though, fear works against us these days. It's our *mind* working against us. Preventing us from being all the awesome things that we can be. It's a small part of our mind asking us the question, even when we are not aware of it, "Can I handle this situation?". Before the conscious part of our mind has a chance to react, it quickly answers the question with "No, I can't handle this situation."
The next time this happens to you, try to be aware of it. Try to be conscious that you can make a real decision here instead of giving in to fear.

Now that we are becoming more self aware of our fears and challenges, we can begin to see through other people's (and more importantly our own) behaviour. We have a better understanding of why we behave the way we do in different situations.

The important thing here is to be completely honest with yourself.

Think about the last time you were angry. Being honest, ask yourself, why was I angry? The first answer may be a superficial reason: *I was angry because the train I was waiting for was running late.* But why were you angry because the train was late? *Because I did not want to be late for work.* Ok. And why did you not want to be late for work? *Because I don't want to be behind on my workload or I don't want to get fired.* Now we're closer to the meat of it. You fear that you might end up being behind on your workload or that you might be fired. These are mental constructs which make this situation (the train running late) into a much bigger deal than it really is. In this situation, these thoughts do not help you. They do not help the train to come any earlier.

Wouldn't it be better if your mind was not cluttered with these useless thoughts leaving you muddled and confused? If you could declutter your mind you would have better clarity and focus. Then you could easily look at alternatives (like catching a nearby bus) or you might remember that today is the day that two of your colleagues are back from holidays so you won't actually be behind on your work after all.

Your negative emotions are caused by fear. Fear of loss (losing a loved one or losing money), fear of failure (not passing that exam or not being hired), fear of rejection (the person who you approached romantically does not reciprocate). There are as many fears as there are things, places and activities. Your mind, if you allow it, will make every fear into something bigger than it really is. That does not serve you. It's your mind working against you. Like any powerful force, your mind can work for you or against you. Fire can cook your food or it can cook you. Electricity can heat your home or it can electrocute you. Water can sate your thirst or it can drown you. Your mind can get you to any wonderful place or position in this world or it can bring you so far down a black hole that you may never climb back out again. The more *conscious* you are of how your mind reacts in challenging situations, the more in *control* you are of how your mind reacts in challenging situations. Don't be motivated by your fears. Be motivated by love. Be motivated by belief in something better for you and better for those around you. But not by fear.

Examples of ways in which fear works against us

- It can cloud our thinking so that we are less effective
- It can cause a person to become hypochondriac (constantly fearing that they are suffering from a serious illness). This makes for a stressful life and it also attracts those illnesses. If you believe something about yourself for long enough you are inviting it to become true.
- It causes over-protectiveness in relationships. Have you ever been over-protective or had a partner who was? This condition shortens the life of relationships because it adds unnecessary stress.
- If you have ever sat an exam or had a job interview and felt nervous before or during it. A little nervousness can be helpful, it can keep us focused. Lots of people sit exams or attend interviews

where they should be performing well but because they are *too* nervous, they don't perform as well as they should based on all the preparation they have done. That's fear again.

- It is used to control people. In some countries and religions it is used to manipulate citizens and followers. If someone uses fear to control or influence you, that person is not your friend. That person views you as inferior and controllable.

- It can be a massive waste of energy.

- If you avoid fear, it chases you.

- Fear limits your potential. It's the voice inside your head saying "I can't handle this situation". That voice is lying to you.

People Who Were Controlled By Their Fear

Here are some extreme examples of people whose minds worked against them. They were all probably motivated by a range of different things including ambition, pride and greed. It is unlikely that love was a motivation for any of them (when I say love, I don't mean romantic love, I mean a love for themselves or a love for humanity). It might seem like a strange way to look at it but if you think about it for a moment, it will make sense. The following individuals' fears dominated their thinking and motivated their actions, maybe not right at the beginning of their infamous careers but at some point it came to the fore. When fear is our primary motive, bad things can happen:

Adolf Hitler (Austria / Germany) - Instigated WWII. Ordered the murder of 6 million jews, gay people, black people, gypsies and others.

Joseph Stalin (Russia) - Ordered the deaths of somewhere between 18 and 60 million people (mostly his own citizens) & starved an entire country (Ukraine).

David Koresh (US) - Founded a cult in Waco, Texas. Culminated in the death of 79 cult members.

Pol Pot (Cambodia) - Between 1 & 3 million people died as a result of his policies as premier of Cambodia.

Osama Bin Laden (Saudi Arabia) - Incited hate and wilful destruction of non-Islamic people and cultures.

Saddam Hussein (Iraq) - Directly ordered the deaths of 200,000 of his own citizens and that was apart from the wars he was involved with.

Kim Il Sung and his son and grandson (North Korea) - All 3 generations have overseen the destruction and depletion of the North Korean people and their land. Wanton cruelty, insane decadence and grossly negligent mismanagement of an entire nation of 20 million people.

Emperor Nero (Rome) - Ordered his own mother's death. Murdered his wife. Grossly mismanaged the Roman Empire.

King Leopold II (Belgium) - In the Congo in Africa he exploited and stole the natural resources and caused the deaths of somewhere between 1 and 15 million Congolese people. His favoured torture method included cutting off the hands of slaves who refused to work.

Idi Amin (Uganda) - Caused the deaths of 100,000 to 500,000 people.

Vlad the Impaler (Romania) - Liked to impale the (still alive) bodies of his enemies on spikes outside his castle to deter potential attackers.

Jim Jones (US) - His 900 cult followers committed suicide at his order.

Heinrich Himmler (Germany) - During WWII he was leader of the Nazi SS, Chief of the German Police and head of the Gestapo. He personally ordered and organised the deaths of about 10 million people.

Many of the above examples were dictators. They had to be ruthless to get to where they were as dictators and they knew that there were many others beneath them who were fully ready to step into their shoes… even if they had to steal them (or even murder the shoes' owner). All dictators make many enemies and eventually (or immediately) they alienate their population. Many experience violent deaths as a result. It is in the nature of a dictator to live in constant fear because they know, under all the showmanship and authoritarianism, that what they are doing it wrong and at some point their world will come crashing down.

All of us at different times in our lives allow fear to dictate what we do. Thankfully few of us become, or even have the opportunity to become, the monsters listed above. But the pain we put ourselves through because of our fears is enormous. Most people around won't see 1% of this pain in others but that doesn't make it any less real.

While fear can help us to gain greater self-awareness, it can also prevent us from being the best versions of ourselves. And in the most extreme cases can even cause us to behave like a dictator!

6. Discovering Your Challenges & Fears

"There is no illusion greater than fear."
- Lao Tzu

Eckhart Tolle once said that phobias are only possible if we are living in the future. If we live in the present, we cannot fear future possibilities.

Many people believe that they have no fears. In most cases however, it is not true. The people who say this, in most cases, are not being truthful with themselves. Admitting vulnerabilities is not an easy thing to do. When I was a teenager, I could not admit any kind of weakness, even just to myself, including a fear of *anything*.

The truth is that it is when we are feeling stronger, when we are feeling more in control that it is easier for us to admit a fear. It takes courage to admit fear.

If you have been hiding from the truth for most of your life (ie. if you are like most people, including me), then you firstly need to consciously discover what your fears are. You do this by trying things you have not tried before. By making a list, similar to a bucket list (let's call it a Challenge List), and start to do those things. Be as honest as you possibly can. This is for your eyes only... Although once you have finished all the parts of this book, I would love for you to share your list with me and with others if you are happy to.

Have a look at the top ten fears, as compiled from an Outside the Comfort Zone Fear survey held at my website www.outsidethecomfortzone.ie. 1,000 people from more than 50 countries have responded to this survey so far as of December 2016.

Below are the 10 most common fears or phobias which people suffer from. Do you experience fear when exposed to any of these things? Spiders? Heights? Public speaking?

1. Glossophobia - Fear of Public Speaking - 37%
2. Acrophobia - Fear of Heights - 35%
3. Arachnophobia - Fear of Spiders - 30%
4. Claustrophobia - Fear of Enclosed Spaces - 25%
5. Nyctophobia - Fear of the Dark - 20%
6. Agoraphobia - Fear of Open Spaces - 11%
7. Cynophobia - Fear of Dogs - 9%
8. Aviophobia - Fear of Flying - 7%
9. Sociaphobia - Fear of Interacting with Others - 6%
10. Necrophobia - Fear of Death - 5%

You may have heard of several or all of these top ten phobias before. In fact, there is a good chance that you have experienced one or more of them at some point in your life.

To give you a clearer idea of just how many things it is possible to have a phobia of, here is a substantial list of fears that people suffer from. Any person, any activity, object, place or situation you can think of, a least one person out there has a fear of it. Some of these fears will seem silly. Others will even seem crazy. But they are all fears that people really do suffer with. I want you to highlight any items which you know you are afraid of and also highlight the items which you honestly do not know whether or not you are afraid of. Be as honest as you possibly can. This is for your eyes only.

Ablutophobia- Fear of washing or bathing.
Acarophobia- Fear of itching or of the insects that cause itching.
Acerophobia- Fear of sourness.
Acousticophobia- Fear of noise.
Acrophobia- Fear of heights.
Aerophobia- Fear of drafts, air swallowing.
Aeroacrophobia- Fear of open high places.
Aeronausiphobia- Fear of vomiting secondary to airsickness.
Agateophobia- Fear of insanity.
Agliophobia- Fear of pain.
Agoraphobia- Fear of open spaces or of being in crowded, public places like markets. Fear of leaving a safe place.
Agraphobia- Fear of sexual abuse.

Agrizoophobia- Fear of wild animals.
Agyrophobia- Fear of streets or crossing the street.
Aichmophobia- Fear of needles or pointed objects.
Ailurophobia- Fear of cats.
Albuminurophobia- Fear of kidney disease.
Alektorophobia- Fear of chickens.
Algophobia- Fear of pain.
Alliumphobia- Fear of garlic.
Allodoxaphobia- Fear of opinions.
Amathophobia- Fear of dust.
Amaxophobia- Fear of riding in a car.
Ambulophobia- Fear of walking.
Amnesiphobia- Fear of amnesia.
Amychophobia- Fear of scratches or being scratched.
Anablephobia- Fear of looking up.
Ancraophobia- Fear of wind. (Anemophobia)
Androphobia- Fear of men.
Anemophobia- Fear of air drafts or wind.(Ancraophobia)
Anginophobia- Fear of angina, choking or narrowness.
Anglophobia- Fear of England or English culture, etc.
Angrophobia - Fear of anger or of becoming angry.
Ankylophobia- Fear of immobility of a joint.
Anthrophobia or Anthophobia- Fear of flowers.
Anthropophobia- Fear of people or society.
Antlophobia- Fear of floods.
Anuptaphobia- Fear of staying single.
Apeirophobia- Fear of infinity.
Aphenphosmphobia- Fear of being touched. (Haphephobia)
Apiphobia- Fear of bees.
Apotemnophobia- Fear of persons with amputations.
Arachnephobia or Arachnophobia- Fear of spiders.
Arithmophobia- Fear of numbers.
Arsonphobia- Fear of fire.
Asthenophobia- Fear of fainting or weakness.
Astraphobia or Astrapophobia- Fear of thunder and
lightning.(Ceraunophobia, Keraunophobia)
Astrophobia- Fear of stars or celestial space.
Asymmetriphobia- Fear of asymmetrical things.
Ataxiophobia- Fear of ataxia. (muscular incoordination)
Ataxophobia- Fear of disorder or untidiness.
Atelophobia- Fear of imperfection.
Atephobia- Fear of ruin or ruins.

Athazagoraphobia- Fear of being forgotten or ignored or forgetting.
Atomosophobia- Fear of atomic explosions.
Atychiphobia- Fear of failure.
Aulophobia- Fear of flutes.
Aurophobia- Fear of gold.
Auroraphobia- Fear of the Northern lights.
Autodysomophobia- Fear of one that has a vile odor.
Automatonophobia- Fear of ventriloquist's dummies, animatronic creatures, wax statues - anything that falsely represents a sentient being.
Automysophobia- Fear of being dirty.
Autophobia- Fear of being alone or of oneself.
Aviophobia or Aviatophobia- Fear of flying.
Bacillophobia- Fear of microbes.
Bacteriophobia- Fear of bacteria.
Ballistophobia- Fear of missiles or bullets.
Bolshephobia- Fear of Bolsheviks.
Barophobia- Fear of gravity.
Basophobia or Basiphobia- Inability to stand. Fear of walking or falling.
Bathmophobia- Fear of stairs or steep slopes.
Bathophobia- Fear of depth.
Batophobia- Fear of heights or being close to high buildings.
Batrachophobia- Fear of amphibians, such as frogs, newts, salamanders, etc.
Belonephobia- Fear of pins and needles. (Aichmophobia)
Bibliophobia- Fear of books.
Blennophobia- Fear of slime.
Bogyphobia- Fear of bogeys or the bogeyman.
Botanophobia- Fear of plants.
Bromidrosiphobia or Bromidrophobia- Fear of body smells.
Brontophobia- Fear of thunder and lightning.
Bufonophobia- Fear of toads.
Cacophobia- Fear of ugliness.
Cainophobia or Cainotophobia- Fear of newness, novelty.
Caligynephobia- Fear of beautiful women.
Cancerophobia or Carcinophobia- Fear of cancer.
Cardiophobia- Fear of the heart.
Carnophobia- Fear of meat.
Catagelophobia- Fear of being ridiculed.
Catapedaphobia- Fear of jumping from high and low places.
Cathisophobia- Fear of sitting.

Catoptrophobia- Fear of mirrors.
Cenophobia or Centophobia- Fear of new things or ideas.
Ceraunophobia or Keraunophobia- Fear of thunder and lightning.(Astraphobia, Astrapophobia)
Chaetophobia- Fear of hair.
Cheimaphobia or Cheimatophobia- Fear of cold.(Frigophobia, Psychophobia)
Chemophobia- Fear of chemicals or working with chemicals.
Cherophobia- Fear of gaiety.
Chionophobia- Fear of snow.
Chiraptophobia- Fear of being touched.
Chirophobia- Fear of hands.
Chiroptophobia- Fear of bats.
Cholerophobia- Fear of anger or the fear of cholera.
Chorophobia- Fear of dancing.
Chrometophobia or Chrematophobia- Fear of money.
Chromophobia or Chromatophobia- Fear of colors.
Chronophobia- Fear of time.
Chronomentrophobia- Fear of clocks.
Cibophobia- Fear of food.(Sitophobia, Sitiophobia)
Claustrophobia- Fear of confined spaces.
Cleithrophobia or Cleisiophobia- Fear of being locked in an enclosed place.
Cleptophobia- Fear of stealing.
Climacophobia- Fear of stairs, climbing, or of falling downstairs.
Clinophobia- Fear of going to bed.
Clithrophobia or Cleithrophobia- Fear of being enclosed.
Cnidophobia- Fear of stings.
Cometophobia- Fear of comets.
Coimetrophobia- Fear of cemeteries.
Coitophobia- Fear of coitus.
Contreltophobia- Fear of sexual abuse.
Coprastasophobia- Fear of constipation.
Consecotaleophobia- Fear of chopsticks.
Coulrophobia- Fear of clowns.
Counterphobia- The preference by a phobic for fearful situations.
Cremnophobia- Fear of precipices.
Cryophobia- Fear of extreme cold, ice or frost.
Crystallophobia- Fear of crystals or glass.
Cyberphobia- Fear of computers or working on a computer.
Cyclophobia- Fear of bicycles.
Cymophobia or Kymophobia- Fear of waves or wave like motions.

Cynophobia- Fear of dogs or rabies.
Cypridophobia or Cypriphobia or Cyprianophobia or Cyprinophobia -
Fear of prostitutes or venereal disease.
(phobialist.com)

… and they are only the phobias whose words begin with the letters A, B or C. Now you can see what I'm talking about when I say that phobias or fears can be of anything you can possibly think of… even baby unicorns.

Challenges and fears go hand in hand. If you overcome a challenge, you will have also overcome at least one fear, maybe several fears. At the minimum you will have overcome fear of failure.

At the beginning of this chapter I mentioned a Challenge List that I have been using for a few years. Here is a sample of items from my Challenge List (with a few other challenges thrown in the mix). I want you to see them both for ideas to get your list started but also to illustrate just how varied and random your own list can be. Make sure to include experiences on your list too - countries you want to visit at some point in your life, things you want to be involved with and skills you want to learn. You may have many opportunities to do items on the list below. Some of them you might have a once-off opportunity to do. Recognising that opportunity and then taking it is something you get better at the more you do it.

Learn a foreign language
Quit using a computer for all non-essential tasks for a week
Quit fast food for a month
Go to a rock concert
Go to a music festival
Participate in a protest
Learn how to roller skate
Learn how to say "thank you" in 50 languages
Write a song
Bungee jump
Go a carnival in Rio de Janeiro

Smoke a cigar in Cuba
Create a website
Build your family tree
Make a decision (if there's something you've been delaying making a decision on)
Be honest with yourself
Be rejected by a romantic interest
Kiss a stranger on New Year's Eve
Keep a diary
Get into good physical shape
Get a tattoo
Donate Blood
Have a suit made by a tailor
Plant a tree
Anonymously give to a charity
Fart in a crowded place
Make a speech in public
Cook a complex meal
Learn how to blow bubble gum
Learn to draw human anatomy
Kiss in the rain
Sing karaoke
Learn to read a compass
Learn to tie 10 knots
Solve a Rubiks Cube
Write a book
Build a sandcastle
Write your will
Swim with dolphins
Have babies
Phone typing speed 55wpm
Learn Java coding
Learn PHP coding
Kiss a stranger in a bar
Take photographs and sell them
Dance naked
Witness a birth
Experience 24 hours of constant sunlight
Jump on a trampoline
Watch fireworks from the roof of a building
Save someone's life
Scuba dive

Climb a mountain
Create an original cartoon character
Sleep in an ice hotel
Sell a piece of art created by yourself
Organise your music
Have a full conversation with a telemarketer
Visit the Eiffel Tower
Send a message in a bottle
Ask someone you have just met to go out on a date
Sleep under the stars
Ask your boss for a pay rise
Invent a cocktail
Paint graffiti
See the Sahara Desert
Take a year off work
Make a short film
Fly first class
Talk to God
Meet your hero
Shave your head completely (blade zero)
Get a STI / STD test
Refuse to pay for a bad meal
Win an award
Milk a cow
Stand at the edge of a volcano
Learn to play an instrument well
Find a career that you truly enjoy
See a lunar eclipse
Shoot a gun
Invent something
Try paintball
Win the lottery
Teach someone illiterate to read
Own a dog. Teach it cool tricks
Be free
See Jerusalem
See Mecca
See the birthplace of Buddha
Learn to take good photos
Influence someone famous
Do stand up comedy in front of a large audience
Stay on a desert island

Learn to drive (get full license)
Learn to meditate well
Try yoga
Run a half marathon
Run a marathon
Run an ultramarathon
Sing in a choir
Go camping by bicycle
Win a short story competition
Repair a bicycle puncture
Replace a car tyre
Repair a common car engine problem
Gain 1000 subscribers on your own Youtube channel
Try a meditation retreat
Learn First Aid
Learn to Code Python
Learn to draw
Learn a card trick
Learn a coin trick
Learn a cash note trick
Shower in a waterfall
Make an origami crane
Learn to lucid dream
Hold a spider
Hold a snake
Eat insects
Catch a fish
Gut a fish
Draw something good enough to hang on a wall
Learn to do a party trick
Bake a cake
Create a treasure map and hide treasure and clues
Learn to swim well
Learn to juggle
Sing solo in front of an audience
Be vegetarian for a week
Typing Speed 80 wpm
Make a model airplane
Learn HTML/CSS
Have a spend nothing day
Forgive your siblings
Write your ideal cv

Join a Toastmasters club
Learn bush craft
See Iceland
Learn the countries and capitals of the world
Learn the NATO Phonetic Alphabet
Learn to tie a bowtie
Learn how to jump start a car
Learn how to verbally tell a good story
Learn how to whistle
Switch off your phone for 24 hours
Learn a memory trick
Learn to do a handstand
Learn how to tumble
Balance on one foot for 15 minutes
Give up sugar for a predetermined period of time
Fast completely for one day (24 hours)
Fast completely for 2 days (48 hours)
Write a blog post for a public blog
Use a flotation tank
MC an event
Walk on hot coals
Eat jellyfish
Eat a scorpion
Start your own business
Compete in an obstacle course race
Eat ostrich
Eat kangaroo
Try quad biking
Visit Skellig Michael
Cycle the Ring of Kerry
Handle a swarm of bees
Try speed dating
Try blind dating
Try babysitting
Plant a flower
Try ballet
Try caving
Overcome your weakest subject in school
Understand yourself better by asking yourself questions and
challenging yourself
Figure out algebra
Learn to drive

Go back to college
Take an exam
Travel by airplane
Cook something new
Have that difficult conversation with someone close to me
Book that dental appointment... and show up on the day!
Say "No" when you would usually say "Yes" but you know it doesn't work for you
Say "Yes" when you would usually say "No" but you know it doesn't work for you

*Always take the necessary precautions when taking on a challenge. Some require little or no precautions, some require extreme caution. If you are uncertain, seek professional guidance.

If there are items on the Challenge List above that you are not familiar with, step outside your comfort zone by looking them up and then try them!

Not everything on the Challenge List suits everyone. Some of the suggestions won't suit vegetarians. Some of the suggestions cost money that you may not have right now. Some of them are things you may only get the opportunity to do once in your life. The Challenge List above is just to get you started. Take what you want from it.

The list of challenges above is a long list, but nothing compared to how long your own list will be in the near future. I included this long list because I want to emphasise just how many different ways we can step outside of our comfort zones. Not just the obvious things normally associated with bucket lists (although climbing mountains and entering races are excellent challenges too!).

Now start on your own lists. Write down any challenges and fears which come to mind. Two columns: One for fears (beginning with the ones you highlighted on the Fear List above) and one for challenges.

By starting the Fear List, you will be more self-aware regarding your fears. This puts you at an immediate advantage. Now you can begin to conquer them. In chapter 7 we will look at exactly how to conquer them. Once you have done that, you will have NOTHING in your way. Nothing preventing you from becoming or achieving whatever it is that you want. Any objects, any place, any situation, any physical, emotional or mental condition, any person: All of these things have been feared at some point by someone. Anything and everything can be a subject of fear.

The Challenge List will help you to maintain momentum in the coming weeks and months.

Take ideas for both columns from the lists above. You can also check phobialist.com or www.outsidethecomfortzone.ie for more ideas.

… but that's just the beginning. I want you to add to your list every time you think of something new.

Starting right now, today, begin to approach the fears which you have highlighted. You'll discover soon enough whether or not they really are fears or challenges for you. In the process of trying these things, you will probably overcome some of them, just by facing them. So don't be too surprised if you have fears on your list which you discover you have and at the same time you have begun the process, or even completed the process, of overcoming them.

Do it today.

7. Overcoming your Challenges & Fears

*"Do the thing you fear to do and keep doing it…
that is the quickest and surest way
ever yet discovered to conquer fear."*
- Dale Carnegie

How do we overcome our fears? It's not rocket science but it takes commitment.

Now that you have the beginnings of your Challenge List and your Fear List it's time to get down to the work.

On each list I want you to highlight the challenges and fears where no physical, emotional, psychological, financial or any kind of real danger is present. These will be the first challenges and fears that you will conquer. If you don't highlight any, that's not a problem. Just start with what you perceive to be the easiest ones. As your confidence grows you will take on tougher and tougher challenges and fears.

Put simply, there are 3 ways to overcome challenges and fears:

1. You outgrow them without any effort. This is common with something like fear of darkness. Many of us are lucky enough to outgrow it without even really trying.

2. You jump straight into the challenge. If your fear is not too intense, this is the most effective and quickest way to overcome your fear.

3. When your fear is more intense, the wise thing to do is spend more time in preparation. I was petrified in the days and weeks

running up to the first talk I ever gave to large audience. The single most effective way to reduce my fear was preparation. I focused my attention on researching and preparing and practicing. Prepare and, if necessary, take gradual, small steps towards it.

All three ways to overcome challenges and fears become easier (they can even become effortless) the more that you step outside of your comfort zone.

Use these tips to overcome your challenges and fears.

- Speak to someone who is not afraid of it. They might have an enlightening opinion of it.
- Learn more about the thing that you fear. The more you know the less scary it is. Remember, underlying all fears is the fear of the unknown.
- Don't waste your time lingering on *why* you have a specific fear. It may be interesting and even helpful for you to discover why. But over the long term it is unlikely to be helpful if you keep going back to it again and again.
- Find someone you can trust and speak with them about it. Speaking out loud will diminish your fear.
- Work up to it slowly. Prepare. Prepare. Prepare.
- Try your best to be conscious of when your mind reacts in fear. Just being aware of how you react in different situations can have an enormous positive impact on how you will react the next time.
- While it is wise to prepare in cases of possible real danger, it is also essential to focus most of your attention on right here, right now. Don't make the mistake of thinking too many steps ahead and of all the terrible possibilities which *might* occur.

Use all the information above but also remember this: The more challenges and fears that you overcome, the more confident you become in dealing with new challenges and fears. You become that ever growing snowball rolling down the mountain. You become that relentless unstoppable force.

But to really take control of your situation, make sure to complete the Outside the Comfort Zone System at the end of this book.

There is always hope. There's always a chance of life becoming better for you. The night is often darkest just before the dawn.

8. My Story

I survived an accident which caused a serious medical illness for two years and turmoil in my life for many more years. My story is not such an unusual one. Many people have suffered in far greater ways than I have.

I feel extremely lucky in that I have not only recovered from a serious injury but I have also learned a valuable lesson in the process.

Having such a wonderful and supportive family has made this whole journey so much easier. I am so, so grateful to them.

I had a spell of a few years when I was a child where I was sick a lot of the time. I spent a large portion of 3rd class of primary school (age 8) in and out of hospital. I had epilepsy, asthma, extreme lethargy, eczema and other conditions which made life challenging for me and for my parents. For a lot of my childhood and teenage years I had the appearance of not having slept properly. I had a pasty white face, deep shadows under my eyes and an unusually skinny frame.

Because of all these medical issues, I learned that the wisest way for me to approach everything in life was to do it carefully, very carefully. I unconsciously decided to not take risks. This approach continued for many years, until I was in my late twenties. I chose to study what I perceived to be the easiest subjects in school. I chose them so I was more likely to pass. Except for a short and unconvincing stint playing rugby, I avoided contact sports. I didn't approach girls that I liked because they might have rejected me. I became obsessive about risk avoidance. I didn't realise any of this until years later.

Looking back now, I have concluded that living in this risk averse way caused me 1) to lose friends and girlfriends, 2) to give people a negative impression of me and 3) to miss out on countless opportunities.

1) Losing friends and girlfriends: I was careful in most of my friendships and relationships to not let the other person know how important they were to me. In my mind at that time, it would have given the other person power if they had known how important they were to me. If they ignored or left me, I would have suffered. The truth is that when they did finally ignore or leave me, I suffered anyway. And they always did leave because they consciously or unconsciously sensed that I was not fully giving myself to the friendship or relationship.

2) With new people: who I met through friends, work, school or university I always played it cool. Which worked for a while. While these people were getting to know others they met at the same time they had met me, my friendship with them was frozen in the early, superficial stages. It would never move beyond that because I was afraid of moving beyond that. I didn't want to ever have to rely on any of these new potential friends too much.

3) I have had many opportunities in my life up until this point. Some of them came about because I am lucky that I was born in a first world country. Some of them because of friends and family and some because I created the opportunities myself. But in many of these situations I squandered the opportunity.

When I left college I played it safe by taking a job in banking. Not everyone had the same experience of banking. It would unfair and inaccurate to say that all banking roles are boring or too safe. But the particular roles I worked at in banking were insanely boring for me but also safe. I took home a salary. I spent my salary on food, bills, girlfriends, clothes, rent.... I was living the most unremarkable life you can imagine. Not just externally but internally too.

Where Things Went Wrong

The Celtic Tiger (Ireland's brief few years of extreme economic prosperity) came to an end in 2008 as the worldwide recession began. I had been working for a bank selling loans to private customers. I had been earning a living but I knew it was not a career. Not for me. When the recession hit, I decided to move to another area in banking which was not reliant on sales commission to make up a half-decent salary. I got a job with a corporate bank which paid a flat salary. But in time I realised that I had not made a good choice. I thought it was a shrewd choice at first but it ended up nearly killing me.

I found the work just as boring as the previous banking role but this time there was so much more pressure and so many more things to learn, things on which I had no point of reference before beginning the job. And, did I mention it was boring? It was so boring it would bring tears to your eyes. Doing that work was deeply soul destroying. Knowing that you were working long days and being exhausted when you get home but knowing that all your work, all your time, all your effort was in vain. It was heart-breaking. To be balanced with my description I should mention that not everyone experienced it in the same way.

For a few years I was struggling with life. My job was insanely dull yet somehow also extremely stressful. It consisted of large sums of (albeit imaginary) money being moved around from one location to another. There was little room for error. The workload always seemed to be out of control. I was constantly chasing my tail: Coming into the office earlier and leaving later. I was wearing myself out. I became exhausted over time. Exhaustion exacerbated my anxiety. Anxiety fed into more exhaustion. It was a vicious cycle. For a long time I did not take lunch breaks because I could not justify taking them with such a massive outstanding workload. Many of my colleagues were in a similar situation. I may have ended up working in banking for much longer if I had not been blessed with severe brain trauma.

Stress took over my life. My health and outlook on life deteriorated to the point that I felt hopeless. Endlessly clocking in the hours from one day to another, always exhausted and waiting only for the next chance to rest and sleep. My thinking was dulled. My enthusiasm for life was non-existent. My health was at a catastrophically low level.

One sunny Friday evening, June 18th 2010, I was on the way home from the office about to start my two weeks holidays when it finally happened. I lost consciousness and collapsed. My head hit the ground hard. The kind man who phoned for the ambulance and waited with me until it arrived told me later that he had asked me where I live. I responded by naming several nearby areas. I couldn't decide where I lived. I must have been in a bad way. I blacked out again. I woke up hours later in the Accident and Emergency Department of St. Vincent's Hospital in Dublin. A few hours later I checked myself out thinking that I was ok. Or as ok as I could be in the stressed and exhausted condition that I was in. It was five days later when I first encountered vertigo. It lasted for two hours that time but the condition stayed with me for five years.

My Experience of Brain Trauma

The brain trauma that I incurred that day left me out sick from work for the next two years. I believe that the damage done to my brain was complicated by the level of stress and exhaustion that I was dealing with. When I tried to return to work at the end of the two weeks of holidays, I lasted only a few hours. My symptoms rendered me incapable of being in an office environment or doing any kind of work.

I had two years of daily headaches, exhaustion, hearing sensitivity, light sensitivity, memory loss and goldfish-level of mental focus. I also had a lot of trouble balancing. I kept falling over when I tried to stand, walk or sometimes even when I was sitting down. It took a long time to figure out the cause of it.

The headaches were exhausting. They pounded through my skull most hours of every day for the first few months. It sapped my energy. I slept as much as I could. I began carrying ear plugs and sunglasses everywhere I went because of my acute hearing and light sensitivity. I looked like a weirdo walking around supermarkets with my sunglasses and earplugs in. At the time it was not funny to me but looking back now I laugh at how I must have looked.

Before all this I used to be a heavy reader. If I was on public transport, which I used a lot preceding my brain trauma, I was always reading. And before bed. And during breakfast. And during lunchtime. During my recovery my focus was abysmal. I couldn't read a paragraph of a book without forgetting what the previous line had been. I realised that there were large amounts of information that I could not remember. That alarmed me. Since recovering, I still sometimes have a weakened ability to remember new information. I have to work harder to remember than I did in the past. I have found that taking more notes and using memory palaces work well for improving memory.

One other symptom became clear after a few months. My social skills were suffering. I was having trouble reading facial expressions or telling whether someone was happy or sad or angry. In conversation with someone, I only had the core information of the words they were speaking. In the past I would have, like most other people, read into their facial expressions too.

Because of all of these symptoms I've described above, interacting with others became challenging. Even though my friends and family knew that I had brain trauma, I think it was difficult for them to understand what I was going through. There were countless times when I was speaking with friends, family and others where I just didn't have the focus to maintain a normal conversation. The result was that people, even sometimes my friends, just thought I was behaving weirdly or that I was not interested in what they were saying. For example, if my focus dipped near the end of something that a friend was telling me, it might return just after they had finished speaking. So now I have someone looking at me expectantly. They may have just made a joke or they may have just asked me a question. I had no idea. In some cases I laughed, as if my friend had said something funny. I guessed wrong, they had not made a joke. They would look at me strangely and then, understandably, treat me differently from there on. I couldn't blame them. But it was so frustrating. It really got to me.

There was a while when I thought I might have low blood pressure. It was because I felt weak all the time. So I bought a blood pressure measurement device. I monitored myself several times every day. My blood pressure was low but I don't believe it was dangerously low. One day I was going for a walk with my parents. There were a few cattle grids at different points along the pathway. These cattle grids make a loud noise when a car drives over them. I had taken out my ear plugs because we were walking in the countryside but I had forgotten about the cattle grids. A car roared over a cattle grid as we stood nearby. The pain that I experienced at that moment was unlike anything I had ever felt before. It felt like a drill penetrating my skull. In frustration at my situation, at the craziness of feeling so much pain from such a minor thing, I threw my backpack on the ground and screamed. I think I frightened my parents… sorry guys. The blood pressure device had been inside the bag. The screen was smashed, it was broken.

But the worst part of, or maybe it's just the part that is the freshest in my memory since I had it longer than the other symptoms, was vertigo. Lots of people suffer from vertigo. Some are good at handling it. They just wait it out. I struggled with it. I resisted it. Every time it happened, or almost happened, I was reminded of that day when I collapsed. It terrified me. Vertigo stayed with me for longer than any of the other symptoms. For the first year that I delivered my Outside the Comfort Zone talk I experienced vertigo every couple of months. I remember the neurologist had spoken about the aura. This is the moment before collapsing or having a seizure when you feel that something is not right. I had felt the aura just before I had collapsed and experienced brain trauma. I felt that same aura at least once during every single presentation I gave in the first year, it freaked me out. It made me sweat heavily because the idea of the same thing happening again: Vertigo, leading to losing consciousness, leading to brain trauma, leading to more wasted years of recovery. I was lucky that I was usually able to find a place to lie down when vertigo struck.

During those two years of recovery from brain trauma I was outside my comfort zone every moment of every day. My symptoms meant that social situations, being outdoors and anything requiring focus were huge challenges.

I was angry at myself too. I might have avoided all of this if I had changed job or even career sooner. I had felt pressure to stay where I was because the recession had begun just a few months after I started working there. I had stuck it out, thinking that things could only improve. I had made the biggest mistake of my life. The incredible thing is that all of this pain was a blessing in the end, a blessing in disguise. At the time it didn't feel like a blessing. At the time I thought I was a goner. I thought I was permanently brain damaged.

I met with many different doctors in the first year but was offered no solution. I returned to St. Vincent's Hospital five times over the first few weeks. I had a battery scans done including CAT, MRI and EEG. My local doctor referred me to a neurologist. I went to a physiotherapist, a neurosurgeon, a psychologist, a psychiatrist and a few alternative healers. Almost all of them were brilliantly intelligent people but overall they could not help me. They could not tell me what exactly was wrong. They could not tell me how to fix it. They could not tell me when, or if, I would recover fully. In the early days of recovering from brain trauma I was even more tired than I had been before it happened. I slept for large parts of the day. I learned afterwards that this is one of the best things you can do to help your brain tissue recover from damage.

I am forever grateful to both of my parents for their support during this time. They went out of their way to help me. They did this even though it was difficult for them to understand what I was going through. It was difficult for all of my family and friends to understand. Partly because they had not experienced brain trauma themselves and partly because due my brain trauma, I had trouble describing to them what I was going through.

After a year, I had lost hope of ever fully recovering. Then my awesome father made a discovery.

While chatting with a friend, he first heard the term "vestibular imbalance". He described it to me: The vestibular canals reside in the ears. They manage our sense of balance so that we do not fall over when we walk or stand or even sit. When someone has too much to drink, their vestibular canals tend to fail temporarily, until they sober up. It seemed to describe my inability to walk, stand up or even sit without falling over. We discovered that a vestibular imbalance specialist was based nearby. That specialist was Aine O' Neill. She was an enormous help. Finally I knew why I had been struggling to balance for so long: My vestibular canals had not worked effectively since I hit my head. People had thought I was drunk because I had so much trouble balancing… even when sitting down. It finally made sense.
The VRT (Vestibular Rehabilitation Therapy) exercises and tests she ran me through improved my condition swiftly.

For the first time I felt hope that I might recover.

I did the exercises that Aine had prescribed for me throughout each day for months. As my ability to balance returned, a sense of control returned too. I sense that I might be able to recover from my other symptoms too. But there was still some time to go before I would be fully recovered. I was still way outside of my comfort zone in everyday situations.

Soon I realised that I could consciously decide to step outside my comfort zone instead of allowing myself to be pushed outside of it. With this realisation I began to compile a list of goals. It was like a bucket list. But I called it my Challenge List. At first it was the simple stuff. Things that many of us, including me, take for granted: Going outside the house, reading a book, meeting a friend, walking on a footpath beside a road. These activities terrified me. At that time in my recovery, they were the equivalent of climbing a mountain or handling a dangerous snake because of my symptoms. In the first 3 months, leaving the house was something I only did if I was going to see a doctor. The risk of encountering loud noises, bright lights or crowds of people was too great a risk for me to take.

After a while I stepped it up a gear. I started going on dates. I did not tell any of the women I dated at this time that I had brain trauma. I wanted to see if I cope with a date without them realising that I was in recovery. I'm not sure to this day if I managed to convince any of them of this. I'm sure they all had a sense that I wasn't one hundred percent. I remember a few of the dates where I would be going to the bar to grab some drinks for us (being Ireland, the pub is still the most socially acceptable location for a date). I remember struggling to retain my balance. I had to lean on the bar, pretending to be casual about it but in reality so relieved to have something to lean on. The real challenge was carrying the drinks back to the table. Trying not to fall over or spill the drinks. With intense concentration I succeeded most times but I must have looked hilarious, staggering across the floor, my eyes darting around at the furniture and carpet, trying to assess distance and my own balance without the help of my vestibular canals.

Once I was able to, I began training myself up. I went running, I lifted weights. I wanted to improve my fitness, knowing that improved fitness would help my recovery. One of my doctors told me to train less as I was stressing my body by doing too much. I took his advice but it took effort to follow. I was so focused on getting better I wanted to be in peak physical condition.

My list grew into a list of all the things I had wanted to do during my years in banking but hadn't because of a lack of time and energy or because I had feared the results of doing those things.

I started addressing each item on the list, beginning with the easier items including: Learning first aid, running a half marathon, living without a mobile phone for a week, giving up sugar for two months, going on a silent retreat for ten days, holding a boa constrictor and eating a meal of insects.

As I ticked off each challenge, I noticed that I was hungry for the next challenge. My apprehension for each challenge was manageable. So I kept adding to my list and I kept stepping outside my comfort zone. I found that my productivity, confidence and creativity soared.

After Recovery

After I had mostly recovered, I was asked to deliver a motivational talk at an international conference. One of the items on my Challenge List had been to make a speech to an audience because public speaking is something that has always terrified me.

In one of my first office jobs, soon after finishing college, I had the weekly task of announcing stats and news to the rest of my colleagues in my department. Each time I did it, I remember that one of my legs would shake so much as I spoke that others who were standing nearby would see it and ask me if I was alright.

However, I recognised this chance to speak to an audience as an opportunity for growth and stepping outside the comfort zone. My chosen topic was fear and overcoming fear... by stepping outside the comfort zone. Although I was nervous as hell and I'm sure the talk could have been better, I felt that this was my future. Since speaking at that first conference, I have given talks to audiences all around Ireland, helping them to embrace fear, overcome it and grow in the process.

I have now spoken at schools, universities and events around Ireland. When I delivered my first few talks I did not have a driving license. I grew up and lived in Dublin near public transport so I never felt the need to drive before. But now my new career demanded that I have a driving license. The first year of driving around Ireland was interesting... and challenging. I was way outside of my own comfort zone not only because I was speaking to large audiences but also with driving. Both activities were new for me and they both took all of my energy. I remember returning from talks on the other side of the country in my first year completely exhausted.

Last year I was booked for three talks in one day at a secondary school. I was to deliver all three one after the other to different audiences. Because I was going to have an early start I drove out there the night before and stayed at a B&B. I rose early the next morning, well prepared and feeling good. I arrived at the school with plenty of time to spare... Then I asked the receptionist if my contact at the school was in the building. I was told that there was no one by that name in the school. That's when I realised that I might be at the wrong school. The school that had booked me shares its name with at least two others in different parts of the country. I was at one of the others.

When I finally reached the correct school a few hours later I had missed the scheduled times for the first two talks. The time remaining only allowed me to deliver the third talk and one other extra talk added at the last minute.

Of course mistakes happen to everyone but I felt like I was the biggest idiot in the world that day. The mix up had happened because of my weak memory and the fact that I did not double check. The poor woman who had booked me for these three talks had told me on the phone exactly where the school was but because I had not seen it written down I had not committed it to memory.

I'm glad that I was able to partially recover the situation by getting there quickly and delivering two talks. However I am forever grateful to the teacher who booked me for her patience and forgiveness in such a mix up. I was so deeply outside of my comfort zone in this situation while racing to get to the correct school and also while delivering my two talks. But I know I did the right thing by not giving up. The easiest thing to do would have been to cancel the whole thing. That is what made it such a great lesson for me. I messed up but it was not something that I would forget soon!

Starting with the personal crisis of brain trauma, in the following years I learned so much about motivation and about myself. I first began public speaking under my own direction at Toastmasters (which I recommend to everyone). I then went on to create my business Outside the Comfort Zone including the website and associated content. Giving my first talk was traumatic but I have gone on to give hundreds of talks in hundreds of venues since then. My most recent project was writing this book. As is often the case, this it took much longer than expected but I am thrilled to have finished it.

My presentations and workshops have grown into something much bigger than I ever thought possible. I feel blessed to have come out the other side of brain trauma intact. There are so many people who never recover fully from similar accidents. I am grateful everyday for what I have, what I have learned and the fact that I can pass on what I have learned to others.

From everything I have experienced, I am convinced that we all need to step outside our comfort zones more often and step further outside our comfort zones too. Don't wait for the challenge to come to you. Step forward to the challenge first yourself. Then YOU are in control. Don't let what happened to me happen to you, too.

Your ability to turn a bad situation into a good one. Your ability to come through a difficult situation intact. Your ability to strive when others are struggling. These abilities come from stepping outside your comfort zone. Don't wait for life to maybe or maybe not prepare you for the challenges of the future. Make the decision today to prepare yourself by challenging yourself.

I am still looking for new, exciting challenges on and off the speaking circuit. At my talks I ask my audiences for suggestions for new ways for me to step outside my comfort zone. And now I ask you too. If you have any suggestions please get in touch with me at marc@outsidethecomfortzone.ie

9. People Who Have Stepped Outside their Comfort Zones

"Great fear is concealed under daring."
- Marcus Annaeus Lucanus

In this chapter we are going to look at a diverse group of well known, and not so well known, individuals who have lived remarkable and world-changing lives by stepping outside of their comfort zones.

In fact, if you can think of anyone who is successful at what they do, they have certainly overcome one or many challenges which most of us think we could not overcome. That person probably thought that they could not overcome these challenges at some point too.

Many of these people below will be recorded by history as heroes. It's not because they had rich parents, it's not because they were stunningly beautiful and it's not because they were lucky enough to win the lottery. It's because of what they achieved by stepping outside of their comfort zones. All of these people have overcome fears. In some cases it was fear of failure. In other cases it was fear of death, fear of the unknown and/or fear of change.

Nelson Mandela

"Our deepest fear is not that we are inadequate. Our deepest fear is that we are powerful beyond measure. It is our light, not our darkness that most frightens us. We ask ourselves, 'Who am I to be brilliant, gorgeous, talented, fabulous?' Actually, who are you not to be?"

Lived in poverty in his 20s, lived in prison for 26 years, President of South Africa 1994 - 1999. Modernised and revolutionised his country. Credited with preventing civil war during his reign.

Malala Yousafzai

"I say I am stronger than fear."

Yousafzai stood up to the Taliban when they invaded the Swat Valley in Pakistan. The Taliban had declared that women should not have access to formal learning. Malala defied them by fighting for her right to an education. In response, the Taliban shot her, one bullet entering the left side of her forehead. Miraculously she survived. She went on to speak at the UN and was the youngest ever Nobel Peace Prize nominee.

Thomas Edison

"Many of life's failures are people who did not realize how close they were to success when they gave up."

His teachers told him he was "too stupid to learn anything". Edison failed more than 1,000 times to make a working light bulb. He persisted and succeeded.

Rosa Parks

"I have learned over the years that when one's mind is made up, this diminishes fear; knowing what must be done does away with fear."

Refused to give up her seat to a white person in the coloured section of a bus. Became an important symbol of the civil rights movement in the US and internationally.

Bill Gates

"People always fear change. People feared electricity when we learned to harness it."

Bill Gates failed with his first company Traf-O-Data, a traffic data processing device. Became richest man in the world with Microsoft. Worth more than $90 billion, since retirement he has donated more than $30 billion to less economically fortunate people.

Oprah Winfrey

"Whatever you fear most has no power - it is your fear that has the power. The thing itself cannot touch you. But if you allow your fear to seep into your mind and overtake your thoughts, it will rob you of your life."

Oprah had a difficult childhood. She lived in great poverty. She was sexually abused at an early age. She was demoted from a television job early in her career as a news anchor and told that she "wasn't fit for television". After she took over a daytime talk show, viewership ratings went through the roof. This later led to her own program – The Oprah Winfrey Show. The Oprah Winfrey Show has proved to be one of the most successful and highly watched TV programs of all time. It broke through many social and cultural barriers.

JK Rowling

"It is the unknown we fear when we look upon death and darkness. Nothing more."

Was a single mother in Britain with no income beyond social welfare. She is now world renowned for the Harry Potter book series.

Albert Einstein

"The fear of death is the most unjustified of all fears. There's no risk of accident for someone who's dead."

Unable to speak until age 4, unable to write until age 7, parents and teachers were concerned that he was mentally handicapped and that "he would never amount to much."

Stephen King

"Fear is the emotion that makes us blind."

In frustration with his writing and so many rejections from publishers, King threw his early draft of Carrie into the bin. His wife retrieved it and convinced him to keep at it. He has now sold more than 350 million books.

Jay Z

"Those who are successful overcome their fears and take actions. Those who aren't submit to their fears and live with regrets."

Grew up in poverty in Brooklyn, New York. Is now one of the most successful hip hop artists in the world. Sold more than 100 million records, won 21 Grammys and is worth more than $520 million.

Charlize Theron

"You cannot create anything interesting from a comfort zone. You have to work from a place of fear and failure."

Her father was an alcoholic. She witnessed him attacking her mother and witnessed her mother shooting him dead in self-defence. She is now an Academy Award and Golden Globe Award winning actress and movie producer.

Emily Dickinson

"If your Nerve, deny you - Go above your Nerve - "

Suffered from manic depression. She was a prolific poet. Most consider her to have been one of the most significant poets of the United States.

Stephen Hawking

"I have lived with the prospect of an early death for the last 49 years. I'm not afraid of death, but I'm in no hurry to die. I have so much I want to do first."

Diagnosed with motor neurone disease at age 21 and given a life expectancy of 2 years. He has gone on to make some of the most important contributions to our understanding of cosmology, quantum gravity and general relativity.

Abraham Lincoln

"It often requires more courage to dare to do right than to fear to do wrong."

His fiance died, he suffered several nervous breakdowns, he failed at business and he lost 8 times in elections. He went on to become the 16th president of the US (1861 - 1865).

Mahatma Ghandi

"The enemy is fear. We think it is hate; but, it is fear."

Was leader of the Indian independence movement. He was the first to apply nonviolence in the political field on a large scale.

Michael Jordan

"I have missed more than 9,000 shots in my career. I have lost almost 300 games. On 26 occasions I have been entrusted to take the game winning shot, and I missed. I have failed over and over and over again in my life. And that is why I succeed."

Was cut from his school basketball team. Retired now. Is considered by many to have been the greatest basketball player of all time.

Mark Pollock

Blind since age 22. Since then has completed multiple ultra marathons across ice caps, deserts and mountains. First blind man to reach the South Pole by foot. His legs have been paralysed since July 2010. He continues to achieve great things.

Irena Sendler

Irena risked her life to save 2,500 children from the ghetto in Warsaw in 1942-43.

Ludwig van Beethoven

His music teacher said "As a composer, he is hopeless." His hearing declined from age 28. He was completely deaf by age 44. He continued to compose music until close to his death in 1827. Despite his disability he continued to create world famous music.

Rachel Lee

Holds the Irish record for fastest swim crossing of the English Channel (Male or Female). Had to swim through hordes of jellyfish. As an excellent swimmer she was prepared for the long distance but not for the jellyfish. She pushed on through, outside of her comfort zone.

Joan of Arc

Overcame a patriarchal society's expectations and came to lead the French army to victory at age 18. She was burnt at the stake by her enemies a year later but she has managed to go down in history. Still a well known name more than 500 years later.

-

Nellie Bly

Nellie was an investigative journalist in the late nineteenth and early twentieth century. She broke the world record, at the time, for travelling around the world in 72 days. She feigned insanity in order to be admitted to a mental asylum for 10 days. She wrote a widely read article about the abuse of the asylum patients. This opened the public's eyes to the horrors which occurred in many asylums.

Scott Neeson

Previously president of 20th Century Fox. Left his job to set up CCF (Cambodian Children's Fund). In the process he sold his mansion, Porsche and yacht to fund it. He left the comfort zone of his comfortable life in order to help others.

Bethany Hamilton

Won her first surf competition aged 8. At age 13 her arm was ripped off by a shark while surfing. To the surprise of everyone she returned to surfing within weeks of the accident and has won multiple national and international surfing competitions since then.

Dr. Megan Coffee

An infectious disease specialist who has been working in Haiti since their 2010 earthquake, helping people who have contracted diseases. She gave up a research position at University of California, Berkeley. She stepped outside her comfort zone by risking her health, her finance and her career by leaving the U.S. and coming to Haiti. She receives no salary for her work.

Aran Ralston

In 2003 was trapped by a boulder while hiking. After more than 5 days, he managed to saw off his own arm with a penknife in order to escape. He continues to hike and climb to this day.

Joko Widodo

Indonesian president since 2014. Came from a poor background. Rose to the top of the political elite in the world's 4th most populous country. Widodo must have stepped outside of his comfort zone many, many times to get himself from where he began in life to where he is now, a respected and powerful leader.

There are countless others around the world who don't have as high a profile as the names above but who are living a fully realised life, always venturing outside of their comfort zones.

We can't all be as famous or historically important as the people above but that's not the focus here. The more you challenge yourself, the more you'll see that there are far more important things than being a well known face. The satisfaction of living your life as fully as it can be lived, that's something truly worth fighting for.

10. Step Outside Your Comfort Zone NOW

"Nothing in life is to be feared, it is only to be understood.
Now is the time to understand more,
so that we may fear less."
- Marie Curie

You've gotten this far. Well done. You've already finished the difficult part. Once you have read the next few hundred words, you are ready to start the Outside the Comfort Zone System. You'll be in control. You'll be growing as a person, as a force, in ways you may never have dreamed of before.

If you have been nodding your head as you have been reading this book and thinking, *"Yes, that makes sense"* but then you are continuing on with your life as before, with no change, then you are still remaining within your comfort zone. By taking action, just the process of taking action on the words in this book, you have already begun stepping outside your comfort zone.

To quote the wonderful Susan Jeffers from her excellent book *Feel the Fear and Do It Anyway,(1987)* - *"Everyday do one thing that scares you."*

Do it Today. Every. Day.

It could be something small. Something big. It could be something mentally challenging. It could be something physically challenging. It could be something emotionally challenging. Socially challenging. Spiritually challenging. Take the items from your list and start working through them (maybe you have started already). If you haven't, that's no problem at all. Start now.......

Today.

Do it Today.

I really enjoyed the Matrix movies. Maybe you did too or maybe not. It wasn't their accuracy or the action sequences or the costumes or the acting which grabbed me the most. It was the core idea. It made people rethink how reality works. Reality appears to be fixed. That is the illusion of the Matrix. Reality in fact is a representation of our perception of the world. Everyone's reality is different, sometimes only slightly, sometimes in a massive way.

Now that you have finished reading this book, you have no more excuses to delay.

In the next, and final, chapter you will see an extensive program for increasing your self-awareness, figuring out what you want and getting what you want. It will also get your momentum started to a life of stepping outside of your comfort zone.

To get the most out of it I suggest you start the process right now. But just the first one or two parts for now. Don't overdo it. Give it real thought, get off to a solid start. Come back again the next day to continue the process. Try to complete one or two parts each day for seven days and see how you get on. You don't have to complete it all immediately but please do try to complete it within the next ten to fourteen days while this book is still fresh in your mind.

Start it Today.

Do it Today.

Feel free to get in touch with me at marc@outsidethecomfortzone.ie I would love to hear or read your story just as you have read my story. I want to know where you were at in your life before you decided to take control and where you are now. I want to know what items you have on your own Challenge and Fear Lists and what items you have ticked off so far.

Step Outside your comfort zone now.
Now is the only real thing in this world.
Now is the only thing that truly exists.
Yesterday is history and tomorrow is a mystery.
"I'll do it tomorrow" really means *"I'll never do it"*.

The rest of your life starts today. Even if you are reading these words late at night, do something before you switch out the lights. Do something to show yourself that you CAN do something which you thought you could not.

Amaze yourself every single day by stepping outside your comfort zone every single day. Because you have stuck with this far, I know you can do it.

Do it Today.

Today.

11. The Outside the Comfort Zone System

"Do it today."

The main focus of Do It Today is figuring out your challenges and your fears and overcoming them. As a result, you get the things that you want. You *only* get what you put into it. Any self help book that says otherwise is talking rubbish.

That said, you should take as little or as much as you want from this book. I have used all of the tools that are described below. I used them while I was recovering from brain trauma. They helped me to get out of the funk that I was in. They lit the fire that I needed to get my momentum back and move forward and to be more productive and happy than I had ever been, even before my brain trauma. I have worked with hundreds of audiences using these tools. I have seen amazing leaps in progress for many thousands of individuals using this system. The point is: It works!

Even just *starting* this program may require you stepping outside your comfort zone. Once you have completed this program, you will begin to feel the first signs of that wonderful feeling you get after challenging yourself and realising that you CAN do it. But the point of the program is that you can then go further, go beyond it and use it to your advantage. You can take this journey any direction you want. You are in control.

I have read self help books which offer extremely wise advice, usually something so fundamentally simple yet something we manage to forget about in our daily lives. The only problem with some of these books is that while they offer the best of advice which we can intellectually understand, they do not offer a way for us to REALLY understand their knowledge. This means that every time we read or listen to these books we are reminded and that's fantastic but then in our daily life we cannot implement that knowledge because we only understand it intellectually, not

74

inherently. The Outside the Comfort Zone (OCZ) System solves that problem. Through taking these actions, we can inherently absorb what we need to make the most of ourselves.

I have included a mini version of the OCZ System and a longer, complete version. You might want to jump straight into the complete version. Or you may prefer to try the mini version first, see how it goes and then do the complete version. You decide. Both the Mini and the Complete OCZ System Workbooks are available to download for free at my website www.outsidethecomfortzone.ie. The password is "doittoday". Download the PDF if you want to print it out and fill it in by pen or the Microsoft Word file if you want fill it in on your computer.

I want you to be as honest as possible with yourself when doing these exercises. I also want to be honest with you too. There is something which is usually avoided in self-help books: The effort that you put into these exercises may well vary. If you are feeling energised about doing them, you will do them well and you might do every one of them. Or, like most people most of the time, you will be ready for some but not all of the exercises right now. That's ok. Don't feel guilty about it. Don't feel bad about it. It's normal. The best way to approach these exercises is to read each one's description before doing it. Some will be more useful to you than others (although for most readers, *all* of these exercises are valuable). Do the ones that are most relevant to you first.

Quite often the things that we resist are in fact the things that we really will benefit the most from. So be honest with yourself and do whatever exercises you believe will help you the most (which might be all of them) + remember to challenge yourself: some of these exercises will push you outside of your comfort zone. These exercises are likely to be the most valuable exercises for you.

When I first began travelling around Ireland giving my presentation I was linking the subject of extreme phobias with smaller fears and worries. I was giving guidance on how to overcome our nagging concerns and grab control of our lives. However I realised after a few months that we all sometimes need more than just *"How to overcome our challenges"*. We also need a *"Why?"* As in: *"Why bother overcoming our challenges?"*

What motivates YOU to BE motivated? The answer comes in two parts: 1. The things that you have that you are grateful for and want to keep in your life. 2. The things that you want to bring into your life.

In both parts these can include physical objects, relationships, friendships, concepts, money, states of mind, emotions, mental and physical strengths... the list goes on. The key thing here is to figure out what they are for you. What you are grateful for and what you will be grateful for when you receive it in the future?

You can complete the OCZ System in a paper notebook or digitally on your tablet, phone or computer using the PDF or Microsoft Word workbook if you like. Whatever way works best for you. When I was completing parts of it in the past I used pen and paper but these days I use my phone and computer. When you have completed the program, keep your notepad or digital files/folder so that you can do these exercises going forward on a regular basis.

The Mini Outside
the Comfort Zone System

1. Write down 3 things that are really important to you and why they are so important.
2. Use the life categories listed below and write beside each one a score out of 10 (where 1 is the worst score and 10 is the best). That is your current state in each of these categories. You might want reorder the list of 8 categories below with the most important category for you being at the top and least important at the bottom.

1. Health / Fitness
2. Career / Money
3. Living Environment
4. Family / Friends / Romance
5. Mind
6. Spirit
7. Creativity
8. Personal Development

3. Write down one goal for each of your 8 categories and why.
4. Breakdown each goal into at least 3 parts. These are the steps that you must take in order to reach each goal.
5. Make a Habit Creation Chart (See part 7 of the Complete System below for more details). Some of these habits will be repeated tasks you need to do in order to achieve your goals: Habits such as writing, studying, training etc.
6. Write down 3 self-limiting beliefs. Then write down 3 reasons why each of these beliefs are untrue. (see part 9 of the Complete System below for more details).
7. If you haven't already, start your Challenge List and your Fear List (see chapter 7 and also part 13 of the Complete System for more details).

The first 6 steps above will keep you focused on your goals. Step 7 will spur you on to greater achievement and keep your momentum going.

Remember, you'll find the workbook for the Mini OCZ System at
http://www.outsidethecomfortzone.ie

If you're feeling brave and want to try the Complete Outside the
Comfort Zone System, please continue below...

The Complete Outside
the Comfort Zone System

1. Your Most Important List

What are the most important things in your life? Write them down.
And then write down *why*. Why they are important to you? They will
keep you grounded and provide motivation for taking action.

Examples:

Partner
Parents
Siblings
Children
Career
Friends
Physical Health
Mental Health
Money
Spirituality

Below is a handy way to organise this list with some examples
included:

Most Important Things	Why?
My job	Because I love this type of work + money!
My girlfriend	Because she is the most incredible woman I have ever met and I love her.
Pebbles the Cat	Because he is the best pet I ever had. Fluffy, cute and fun.
My current level of fitness	Because it feels good to be fit.

Keep coming back to this list anytime your motivation wanes. Add and remove from it as you yourself change and the things you care about change. Some aspects of your life will come to the fore. Others will fade away. That's perfectly normal.

"The most important things in life aren't things." - Anthony J. D'Angelo

2. Your Interest List

What inspires or interests you? Start a list. Come back and add to it whenever you find something else. Whenever you have a moment to yourself, look into these things further or give yourself a treat by enjoying these things or things related to them.

For example, here are some of the things I'm interested in…

Space exploration
Fitness
Online marketing
Health news
Writing
Rock music
The meaning of life
Grilled chicken

Come back to this list anytime you need an injection of creativity. The things which you find interesting will always find a way of sparking your creativity.

3. The Where You are at Right Now List

Health/Fitness, Career/Money, Living Environment, Family/Friends/Romance, Mind, Spirit, Creativity & finally Personal Development. Rate them out of ten where 1 is the worst score and 10 is the best. Let's assume that you ultimately want to be at 10 in each category however… it is probably more important to you to be at 10 in some categories than others. You might want reorder the list of 8 categories above with the most important category for you being at the top. We will be returning to these 8 categories throughout the Outside the Comfort Zone System so having them in *your* order of preference will be helpful.

This will help to keep you on track. Update it monthly. You'll always be consciously aware of where you are at if you maintain this list.

4. Your Goals List

Figure out what you want long term. Don't second guess yourself. Don't waste your precious time doubting yourself. Just write down what you want to achieve.

Think in terms of the 8 different aspects of your life as listed here:

1. Health / Fitness
2. Career / Money
3. Living Environment
4. Family / Friends / Romance
5. Mind
6. Spirit
7. Creativity
8. Personal Development (what you are doing right now).

What is the ideal situation for you in each of these categories that would ensure a 10 out of 10 rating for that aspect of your life? Maybe some of the categories are not important to you at all. Maybe you have, right now, the exact idea of what you want in terms of that category. For some categories, you may need some time to figure it out. For those ones, don't stress about it, take your time. But you can begin forging ahead with the others now. As I mentioned before, you might be ignoring a category because you simply don't understand it or you have never in your life before paid attention to it. Consider looking into it. You will be stepping outside your comfort zone by doing this and that is exactly what this book is about. Write at least one goal for each of the 8 categories.

The final part: Write down why you want each of these things. How will it benefit you or those who you care about?

1. Health / Fitness	
Goal	**Why?**
Lose 5kg	Because I will be healthier, feel better & look better

2. Career / Money

Goal	Why?
Attract 50 new clients	Because it will help me to increase my income

3. Living Environment

Goal	Why?
Get to know my neighbours	Because it's a friendlier environment if I know everyone and it's better for security too

4. Family / Friends / Romance

Goal	Why?
Stay in touch more with friends and family	It's important to maintain friendships. Sometimes it takes effort

5. Mind

Goal	Why?
Give brain a rest by switching off tech for 2 hrs every Sunday	To give my brain a rest so that I can function better when I need to

6. Spirit

Goal	Why?
Learn to meditate	I'm not sure but I want to find out

7. Creativity

Goal	Why?
Write a short story	Because I want to challenge myself and learn if I could write a novel at some point in the future?

8. Personal Development

Goal	Why?
Complete the OCZ System for myself	Because I want to be the best version of myself

We all need to be clear about our goals. Without them we just wander aimlessly through life.

"People with goals succeed because they know where they are going." - Earl Nightingale

5. Breakdown of your Goals (The steps to get there)

Start creating breakdowns of each of your goals & put timeframes on them. What tasks should you complete in order to achieve these goals? Some tasks could be done right now, today. Others may take weeks or months or even years. Get them down on your paper or device. Once you have these (and, like all of this program, you can delete or add items at any time), you can use them in the Habits Chart (see exercise number 7). For example: I want to write a book. The breakdown could be: Research, writing, looking for a way to publish, proofreading. But let's focus on research and writing because you need to do a lot of these two things before you even think about publishing. Research and writing can be two new habits for you to cultivate in your habits chart.

Goal	Steps	Deadline
Lose 2kg of weight	Weigh myself	Today
	Make an exercise plan	Today
	Make an eating plan	Today
Attract 50 new clients	Obtain leads and testimonials from existing clients	This week
	Follow phone and email leads	This week
	Advertise a special offer	By Monday

Break down each goal into separate actions. List them in order. Some actions will be once off (so you will copy them to your to-do list). Some will be done every day or every week. Put these ones into your habit chart (explained in the coming pages).

Goals can, and should, be daunting. They should be a big deal. But that can make them intimidating to achieve. The solution? Break them down into the tasks required in order to reach your goals.

Once you have your tasks, you can build them into your To Do List and your Habit Creation Chart. Both are described further below.

"Success occurs when opportunity meets preparation" - Zig Ziglar

6. Your To Do List

"Each day we are born again. What we do today is what matters most." - Buddha

If you're not already doing this, use a To Do list everyday (or 6 days a week if you prefer).

For years, my To Do list was half full with items which I wrote everyday. I was repeating the handwriting and typing the same tasks every day. Leave those things out of your To Do list. They might be things like: Exercise, Tidy Room and Eat Healthy. Your To Do list should instead be things like: Call John about the training schedule, reply to Cassandra about her booking, find a new invoice template etc. The To Do list should be new things each day. Save your daily tasks for our Habit Creation Chart.

Using a To Do list is really a no-brainer. It reminds you of what you need to do and it feels satisfying to cross each item off the list as you do it.

Many people find it more satisfying to cross items off a list on a piece of paper but others prefer to use an app on their phone or computer. Try out both and use whatever works best for you.

Example:

To Do List 28.12.16

1. Call Emily re her email
2. Grocery shopping
3. Gym
4. Get batteries for the torch
5. Reply to those emails about the website
6. Clean the kitchen
7. Hoover the apartment
8. Find a restaurant for next Thursday

7. Your Habit Creation Chart

"What you do everyday matters more than what you do every once in a while."

One of the Founding Fathers of the United States, Benjamin Franklin, had an interesting personal development tool. He called it the virtues chart. It was essentially a spreadsheet where he listed the virtues which he was trying to cultivate. Behaviours which he knew were positive but he did not naturally have. His list included things like Temperance, Frugality, Moderation and Cleanliness. These are all good things to have. However, we're going to use this same concept but for habit creation instead. Almost the same thing, just tweaked a tiny bit.

Create your own Virtues Chart... but for habits. This Habit Creation Chart will help you to develop good habits (some of which can be used to replace bad habits - as someone who has quit smoking, I confirm that this works). The other positive side of using the Habit Creation Chart is that you can remove all those repetitive tasks from your To Do list. This will have another added benefit of making your To Do list more vibrant, with all new tasks on it every day.

Begin by drawing up the following categories as headers for 10 columns on a spreadsheet:

1. Health / Fitness
2. Career / Money
3. Living Environment
4. Family / Friends / Romance
5. Mind
6. Spirit
7. Creativity
8. Personal Development

You may find that some of these categories are not remotely interesting or relevant for you. Include all eight categories anyway. You might discover things about yourself in the coming days and weeks which open up these categories for you. For now, find categories that are relevant for you. Add some of your own if they are not listed above. Maybe Travel could be a category if that's a

88

major part of your life. Or maybe there's some other pastime or hobby that's important to you.

Here are examples of some of the categories and habits that may be relevant for you. Steal whichever ones you want for your own Habit Chart but only use the ones which are relevant for you.

1. Health / Fitness

Run
Ab Training
Squats
Weights
Stand up straight
Eat healthy (feel free to be more specific (5 colours of veg)
Food log
Medical check ups
Sleep earlier
Eat within 30 mins of waking (good for metabolism)

2. Career / Money

Review your budget
Plan how much you need to save
Keep that resume or CV up to date
Network

3. Living Environment

Vacuum
Clean
Repair things

4. Family / Friends / Romance

Appreciate your partner
Show them your appreciation
Surprise them with something THEY like
Make a new friend
Call a friend
Call a relative

Interact on Facebook
Compliment one person

5. Mind

Stimulate your mind in a new way
Brain training
NLP
No 3G or WIFI for one hour
Do your one most important thing first

6. Spirit

Meditate
Pray
Enjoy this moment now
Gratitude notebook
Imitate a spiritual master
Write down 3 goods things that happened today
Consciously let go of worry and regret
Record 3 things that you like about yourself

7. Creativity

Draw something
Write a story or a poem
Paint your home
Create a funny or interesting meme online

8. Personal Development

Review your OCZ System Notebook (paper or digital)
Come back to this book whenever you need to refocus

Now that you have a few short lists of good habits (good habits for YOU, not someone else), you can begin cultivating your habits. Open a spreadsheet. Along the top row list the 10 habits you want to cultivate first. Along the first column (over on the left) list the remaining dates of the current month (the first being today... or tomorrow if you are doing this late in the day). Tick with an X in the boxes beneath for each day that you fulfil that habit. Over time your desired habit will become a normal routine. You will find that you will add and remove new habits as their importance changes for you over time.

Now get started!

For the purpose of layout, this is how part of my habit chart looks as I write these words halfway through the day on 6th Oct.. Remember to tick or "X" off each item as you complete it:

Oct	Gym	Eat healthy	Gratitude 5 Things	Write Book	Call/Txt Relative	Call/Txt Friend	Memory Training
1st	X	X	X	X	X		X
2nd		X	X	X		X	X
3rd	X		X	X	X	X	X
4th	X	X		X	X	X	
5th	X	X	X		X	X	X
6th	X	X	X				
7th							
8th							
9th							
10th							

You might not achieve every single item on your Habit Creation Chart every single day. No problem. You are certainly doing it more often than if you were not using this method.

"We first make our habits, and then our habits make us." - John Dryden

8. Negative Avoidance

"Good things happen when you distance yourself from negative people."

What people, places and activities should I avoid? Be honest with yourself. These are the people, places and activities which you know do not serve you. Be conscious of their existence and the negative effect they have on you. Avoid them wherever possible.

It could be a friend or friends who always complain and have a negative perception of life. It could be a place where you used to live which you have bad memories of. It could be activities such as drinking too much alcohol, smoking cigarettes or eating bad food. Everyone has their own things, people and places to avoid. Be honest and clear with yourself.

Negative Influence	Why?
That cafe around the corner from my apartment	They sell only sugary foods which I know are bad for me
Frank my old friend from school days	He only ever complains about things. I find that I start complaining about things too the more that I spend time with him
Going to nightclubs	It's not healthy for me. The late night and the alcohol that I drink in a nightclub means that I am less productive for 1 or 2 days afterwards

Negative avoidance can seem a little cold when we are referring to people in our lives. However it is necessary step to take in order to be the best version of ourselves. Maybe they will take the hint and improve themselves as a result!

9. Stamp out your self-limiting beliefs

Write down 1 thing that you think you cannot do. Come up with 3 good refutations: Why you actually can do that thing.

Example: Most people I speak with about public speaking say that they are not the kind of person who is good in front of an audience.

In fact, glossophobia (fear of public speaking) is in the top 3 of every top 10 list of phobias that I have seen. It almost always comes in higher on the list than fear of death...

Let's imagine that you also have a fear of public speaking. You think that it is something that you cannot do. Write down 3 reasons why this is not true.

Self-Limiting Belief	Refutations
I cannot speak in front of an audience	1. Many people have done public speaking, even people who are normally considered quiet and shy.
	2. I can speak. All I really have to do is speak a bit louder while standing in front of others.
	3. There was that time when I spoke or shouted in the presence of others and it was fine! No big deal!
I cannot cook	1. I have cooked a meal more than once which others enjoyed
	2. Simple cooking is not rocket science
	3. My friend Martin is able to make a good lasagne so I know I can too
I will never have a good physique	1. I have seen plenty of before and after photos of other people, so it is possible
	2. I have noticed some improvement in just a few weeks so it is fair to assume there will be even more improvement in a few months
	3. I have achieved many other things so I can achieve this no problem

Now do that thing which you thought you could not do. You will completely prove once and for all that your limiting belief was wrong.

10. Your Toolkit

Here are three awesome tools which you can use to get what you want. The more you use them, the better you get at using them.

Visualising

There are some excellent NLP visualisation techniques that you can use to reduce fears and to increase the likelihood of something that you want to happen. They can take some practice but they have been proven to work.

- Take something that you are afraid will happen. Picture it clearly. Hold that image for a moment. Now turn that image black and white, reduce the size of the image and now imagine that image moving away from you, far away into the distance. You feel better about it already don't you?

- We can do the opposite with something that you want. Picture clearly something that you want. Hold the image a moment. Make the image bright and colourful. Make it sparkle. Now make it move, animate it. Bring it closer to you. You may find that you now feel more confident that that situation or experience is going to happen.

Free writing

Free writing is useful for a couple of reasons.

- It can help to de-clutter your mind when you have too many worries and tasks on your mind
- It can give you momentum with a project, creative or otherwise. It gets you going.

The standard way to free write is to grab a notebook and pen and just start writing. Write the first idea that comes into your mind and just follow that thought. You may even discover something about your own opinion or state of mind that you had not acknowledged before.

Positive Affirmations

I used to think that positive affirmations were a stupid idea. They have been mocked in movies and television shows over the years. That's understandable. They can be funny. Plus, it's good not to take ourselves too seriously so why not laugh at them?… But that doesn't mean they don't work. They DO work.

If you feel too self conscious to use affirmations, then don't. Maybe they're not for you. That's ok, we have plenty more tools at our disposal.

You can find affirmations online or you can write your own. What matters is that they are working for you.

Write in the present tense.
Use positive emotion.
It can even be a question. For some this is even more powerful.

Examples:

I am in control of my life.
I am a good person and I am worthy of great things. I deserve the best of everything.
I am an awesome person. I can achieve what I want in all aspects of my life.
How am I so awesome?
How do I look so good?
How come I have so much money coming to me?

Once you have written or found your own positive affirmations, use them at least once a day. This is how you reprogram your mind for what you want.

11. Gratitude

"It is not happy people who are grateful. It is grateful people who are happy."

Every day (morning or evening, you decide) write down 5 things you are grateful for right at that point in time. They can be small things or big things. They can be things that you will always be grateful to have or things that just right at this moment you are grateful for. At first, take some ideas from your first list in the OCZ System: Your Most Important List. Sometimes it's really clear what we can be grateful for. You might have just met someone special or bought a new phone but sometimes we have to dig deeper. It might be something that we usually take for granted such as the fact that we can breathe air or sleep when we are tired or that we have food to eat.

Examples:

I am so grateful for my good health right now. Thank you so much.
I am so grateful for the time that I have to get organised today. Thank you.
I am so grateful for my computer which helps me to get lots of work done. Thank you.
I am so grateful for my friend Bill for his help and support. Thank you so much.
I am so grateful for this nice and warm cup of tea. Thank you.

There is something magical about the effect of gratitude. If you have never practiced it before you may be sceptical. That's natural. Once you try it you will know what I am speaking about. The secret here is to *feel* that *feeling* of gratitude when you are saying or writing your gratitude list.

12. Adjust your expectations

"Adapt to Change Quickly: The quicker you let go of old cheese, the sooner you can enjoy new cheese." - Spencer Johnson (Who Stole My Cheese?, 1998)

Don't be too locked into exactly what results you achieve. If you set a goal to earn €1 million but only earned 90% of that, you'd still be happy right? The purpose of having a clear picture in your mind is to motivate you, to direct you to it. It's easy to lose sight of this. Don't be stubborn about exactly what you will get or achieve.

13. Make your Challenge and Fear List

"Life begins outside the comfort zone." - Neale Donald Walsch

If you have been reading this book from the start, you may have already begun this list. If not, no worries, you can start right now. We can combine them on the below chart.

Every time you overcome a new challenge, everything else will become easier. This is the special ingredient in the Outside the Comfort Zone System. This is what is going to give you the edge that you need. All the other steps are carefully constructed and they really do work. However they can fall apart over time if we lose our focus. Making your Challenge and Fear List and facing your challenges and fears will ensure that you keep your momentum intact.

Not everything has to be a massive undertaking. We can challenge ourselves in so many different ways in every aspect of our lives. Check out chapter 7 for a longer list of examples. The "Why?" column is important. Don't leave it out. Even just writing in "To see if I can do it" is fine. That's a good enough reason.

Here's how your Challenge and Fear List should look. This is a grab of 10 rows of my own challenge list:

Challenge / Fear	Perceived Danger	Why?	Done?
Fear of fainting when donating blood	Low	Fear of fainting since accident	3rd June 2014
Fear of public speaking	Low	Had this fear for a long time. I want to overcome it	28th Feb 2014
Run a half – marathon	Med	Want to see how hard I can push myself over that distance	23rd March 2014
Walk on hot coals	High	Can I do it? I don't know	-
Keep an exercise program for more than 12 months	Low	To see how disciplined I can be	-
Learn to juggle well	Low	I want to know if I can do it	-
Go vegetarian for one week	Low	Not dangerous but I just want to see that I can do it	20th April 2014
Self-assess all aspects of my life	Low	To get a clearer perspective on where I am at	19th December 2013
Try stand-up comedy	Low	To see if I have the courage to do it. I'm not a natural comedian.	16th March 2016

Some more examples of items for your Challenge & Fear Lists:

Some of these will be relevant for you, some not:

Eat a scorpion
Learn how to code
Surfing
Caving
Climbing
Hang gliding
Learn a foreign language
Learn a musical instrument
Start yoga or return to it
Plant a flower
Set goals
Work at your weakest subject in school
Work at the weakest part of your career
Quit sugar for a month

Fear of darkness
Fear of heights
Fear of spiders
Fear of socialising
Fear of flying

14. Self-Awareness Questions

"He who knows others is wise. He who knows himself is enlightened." - Lao Tzu

These are questions we are not often asked by others or by ourselves. Our society does not embrace this level of self-awareness. It is sorely missing for almost everyone. By asking ourselves these questions we force ourselves to think about the most important things in an honest and real way.

Be as honest with yourself as you can bear. You'll get better value the more honest you are.

If any of the previous 13 sections were difficult for you to provide answers for, they might be easier once you have answered these self-awareness questions.

We're going to look at each of the 8 life categories for these questions:
Health / Fitness, Career / Money, Living Environment, Family / Friends / Romance, Mind, Spirit, Creativity & finally Personal Development

1. Health / Fitness

- Do I partake in enough physical activity every week?
- Do I eat healthily every week?
- What do I need to do to correct these things?
- If I am not exercising or eating healthily enough, what does that tell me about how I view myself? Do I not deserve a good quality of life?
- How do I feel about my health and fitness? Good? Bad? Guilty? Excited?

2. Career / Money

- What do I enjoy about my career?
- What do I not like about my career?
- What am I doing to make changes to improve my career for me?
- How can I reduce work-related stress?

- Do I feel satisfied in my work?
- How do I feel about money?

3. Living Environment

- Am I happy with my home and community?
- If not, what can I do about it?
- Do I take care of my home environment?
- Do I make an effort with co-inhabitants and neighbours?

4. Family / Friends / Romance

- Do I feel connected to my partner, friends and family?
- If I do not, how can I strengthen my connections?
- Am I happy with the people who I am closest to?
- Is there anyone who I spend time with who is having a negative impact or influence on me?
- Do I struggle to connect with new people?

5. Mind

- What fears do I have?
- Which of my fears have come true?
- What is my purpose?
- Do I have good mental clarity or is my thinking cluttered?
- What do I like about myself?
- What do I not like about myself?

6. Spirit

- What do I feel passionate about?
- Do I have some kind of belief system? (a religion, personal spirituality, atheism etc.)
- From my own perspective, ask: Am I a good person?
- From the perspective of others, answer honestly, do I think they believe I am a good person?

7. Creativity

- Am I satisfied with how I express myself?

- Do I have some form of creative outlet? (writing, drawing, painting, telling jokes, making music etc.)

8. Personal Development

- Am I challenging and / or improving myself regularly?
- Am I open to learning new things?
- Do I want to be a better person tomorrow?
- How do I handle failure?
- Do I spend time regretting the past or worrying about the future?
- What recurring problems do I have in my life?
- Is there something important in my life (a potential problem maybe) that I am ignoring?

15. Your Ideal Day

Describe your ideal day in the most detail you can. You may not be able to get down the tiniest detail the first time you set about doing this one. Come back it later to add more detail. Your subconscious will work on the finer points while you are focused on other tasks.

- Make sure to include the kind of activities that you enjoy and also the kind of activities that will get you closer to your goals.
- Add in some exact details ie. The brand of coffee that you drink in your ideal day or the type and brand of electronic device that you work on in your ideal day. Start using or obtaining those things now. Start to gradually make your real days more and more like your ideal day.

Example:

6am: Run to the beach for a swim and meditation
7am: Coffee (Killiney Koffee) and breakfast with my partner
8am: Get some work done
10am: A short walk and a snack
11am: More work done
12.30: Lunch with friends
2pm: Back to work, complete big project
4pm: Positive meeting about progress
5pm: Gym
6pm: Dinner in a nice restaurant with my partner
8pm: Arrive at a friend's party
9pm: Party
10pm: Party
11pm: Party
12am: Party
1am: Party
2am: Party
3am: Bed….

By now you should have the following things:

1. Your Most Important List (named as such for two reasons. It includes the most important things in your life and it IS the most important list described in this book)
2. Your Interest List
3. The Where You are at Right Now List
4. Your Goals List
5. Breakdown of Your Goals (The steps to get there)
6. Your To Do List (for once off tasks)
7. Your Habits Chart (for repeated tasks)
8. Negative Avoidance
9. Stamp out Your Self-Limiting Beliefs
10. Your Toolkit: Visualisations / Free Writing / Positive Affirmations
11. Gratitude
12. Expectation Adjustment
13. Your Challenge and Fear List
14. Self-Awareness Questions
15. Your Ideal Day

Stay motivated by referring back to the first 5 parts. Especially No. 1 - Your Most important List.
Stay on track by returning to and updating parts 6 - 15 on a daily or weekly basis. The To Do List and Gratitude List are daily but other parts could be done weekly.

Both the Mini and the Complete OCZ System Workbooks are available to download for free at my website www.outsidethecomfortzone.ie. The password is "doittoday". Download the PDF if you want to print it out and fill it in by pen or the Microsoft Word file if you want fill it in on your computer.

I wish you success with your own OCZ System.

Start today!

You might get so used to being outside your comfort zone that you don't even want to return to it! Now is the time to step forward outside of your comfort zone.

Do It Today!

About the Author

Do It Today is Marc Mulligan's first book. He lives in Dublin, Ireland with his partner Csilla. As an inspirational speaker, Marc gives talks, presentations and workshops about his experiences. He is passionate about encouraging everyone to step outside of their comfort zones. Marc spends much of his free time taking on new ideas, taking on new challenges and taking on the laundry basket.

19661824R00067

Printed in Great Britain
by Amazon